Alfred de Vigny

Alfred de Vigny

BY

ARNOLD WHITRIDGE

LONDON · NEW YORK · TORONTO

OXFORD UNIVERSITY PRESS

1933

MGE

TO
JANETTA

CHAPTER I

L'honneur — c'est la poësie du devoir.

VIGNY

ON THE EVENING OF THE 19TH OF MARCH, 1815, LESS than three weeks after Napoleon had landed with a handful of men in the gulf of Jouan, a gouty old man bundled into a carriage outside the Tuileries and drove quietly out of Paris. Once again the Corsican upstart had cast his spell over the French people, and Louis XVIII had decided wisely, though not perhaps heroically, that he would again retire into exile until his loyal subjects had recovered their sanity. There was something infinitely pathetic about the defence-less old king, driven out of the home of his ancestors and compelled after twenty-three years of exile to expatriate himself once more. The royal household dropped on their knees. " He wears a crown of thorns," exclaimed one faithful old servant. A few of them tried to shout ' Vive le Roi,' but it was no mo-ment for enthusiasm. The King hurried through the crowd. He would like to have been spared this scene: " Children, your devotion touches me, but I need my strength . . . Go back to your families . . . I shall see you again soon." Having finally gained the car-riage he drove off with a large escort of ' gardes du corps.'

The events of the last few weeks had been inexplicable. As soon as he had heard of Bonaparte's return from Elba he had sent his best troops to arrest him. Marshal Ney had even promised to bring him back in an iron cage, but something had happened which no Bourbon could hope to understand. At the sight of their so-called Emperor every one including Ney himself had obviously gone mad. Instead of arresting him they had flung themselves into his arms. It was all very trying but it could be only temporary. Those good men at Vienna, Wellington and Metternich and the Czar Alexander, would never permit this Bonaparte to flout their decisions. They knew just as well as Louis himself that there could be no peace in Europe until that man was sent to some desert island. He would bide his time until the next wave of fate carried him back to the Tuileries.

If these were the thoughts of Louis XVIII as his coach lumbered along the muddy roads of Artois and Flanders they were certainly not shared by the gallant young members of his escort. The Maison du Roi, the bodyguard of the King, which had been hastily reorganized in 1814, was composed of children and old men. The old men had old scores to settle while the young men were intoxicated by the glamour of war. How many times had they not listened to Te Deums of victory and heard the cry of Vive l'Empereur. They had been brought up to the sound of drums, their masters had interrupted their lessons to read them the bulletins of the Grand Army. No wonder they felt ashamed of their youth when an older brother came back from the latest campaign with the Legion of Honor on his breast and his arm in a sling.

"During the wars of the Empire," said Alfred de Musset, "while their husbands and brothers were in Germany, anxious mothers were bringing an ardent, pale, nervous generation into the world." One of these highly strung children was Alfred de Vigny. When the Empire collapsed he had been afraid that there was no future for a man of action, but his mother and father being faithful royalists had managed to get him a commission in the Maison du Roi. He was now embarking on his first campaign, escorting the King into exile. A portrait of him painted at about this time hangs in the Musée Carnavalet. The curly blond hair and the sensitive almost feminine features hardly suggest the warrior, and there is a hint of irony about the lips which is not likely to prove an asset to the professional soldier. But at the age of seventeen, proud of his gorgeous uniform, with a great sabre clanking at his side Alfred de Vigny thought only of the grandeur and not of the servitude of military life. "It had been raining continuously for four days and four nights and I remember that I sang Joconde at the top of my lungs." The spirit of the Grand Army had penetrated the Maison du Roi.

It was not exactly a glorious campaign. After escorting the King as far as Bethune, carefully watched all the way by Bonaparte's lancers, the escort fell back to Amiens, where they were interned until after the battle of Waterloo. That was Alfred de Vigny's first and only experience of active service. How different from the Napoleonic victories he had heard so much about at school, or from his father's campaigns in the Seven Years War that had so fascinated his childhood.

Alfred de Vigny had been introduced to war at an early age. His father's wounds, the family archives, the pictures of his ancestors in coats of mail hanging in the old château in the Beauce, where he used to go for a few weeks every summer — everything spoke to him of war. In his eyes the nobility was a great family of hereditary soldiers, and he determined as a matter of course to fit himself for the trade of his forefathers. "My father's stories of his campaigns," he tells us in an early chapter of 'Servitude et Grandeur,' "combined the profound observation of a philosopher with all the wit and charm of a courtier. Through him I came to be intimately acquainted with Louis XV and Frederick the Great." His father had seen that great man after the battle of Crevelt, where his brother, the eldest of the family, had been killed by a cannon ball. The King had received him in his tent with a grace and a politeness that was 'quite French,' and he had heard him talk of Voltaire and play the flute. Vigny dwells on these recollections because, as he says, "Frederick the Great was the first great man whose character I came to know, and because my admiration for him was the first symptom of my useless love of war, the first cause of one of the most complete deceptions of my life." Poor Alfred! A childish belief in the pomp and circumstance of war was not the only illusion to embitter his career.

ALFRED DE VIGNY

Throughout the Revolution, the Directory and the Empire, Alfred's father, Count Léon de Vigny, had remained a thoroughly irreconcilable royalist. He was the incarnation of the ancien régime, a lingering survival of all that was most charming in eighteenth century society. " He would make me kiss the cross of St. Louis, and pray to God on the feast of St. Louis, thus planting in my heart so far as he was able that love of the Bourbons that possessed the old aristocracy." As a child it never occurred to Alfred to question the righteousness of the monarchy. The almost maternal tenderness of his father, even more than the wit of his conversation, were more than enough to disarm any youthful criticism. As the old gentleman hobbled across the room on his crutches — a bullet through his chest and another in his side, relics of the Seven Years War, had left him partially paralyzed — his son may well have felt that the spirit that could survive the physical agony that he had been forced to endure could be produced only by a race of soldiers steeped in a tradition of service and suffering.

Alfred de Vigny has been charged by many of his biographers with rather exaggerating the importance of his family. Perhaps he does over-estimate the extent of the family possessions but it is always with the intention of proving that his ancestors, rich nobles as they were, have left no permanent mark behind them. He prides himself on being the only one of a bellicose family whose name will be remembered.

ALFRED DE VIGNY

J'ai fait illustre un nom qu'on m'a transmis
*   sans gloire.*
Qu'il soit ancien, qu'importe? il n'aura de
*   mémoire*
Que du jour seulement où mon front l'a porté.

I made illustrious an unknown name.
Ancient it was, but still unknown to fame
Until my genius fanned it into flame.

This is not the pride of an aristocrat so much as the pride of a man of letters. Certainly he was deeply interested in the family history, and he enjoyed analyzing his own character in the light of his ancestors. "Sometimes I seem to feel within myself the different elements of the two races from which I have sprung. My father was from the Nord and my mother from the Midi, the vigorous nerves of the one and the hot blood of the other, combined in such a way as to give me a strong, impressionable nature, perseverant and supple, which I have applied in any direction I wanted, and which has undertaken all the work and endured all the pleasure and fatigue which my imagination imposed upon it. These two strains of noble blood, the purely French strain of my father, hailing from the Beauce, and the Roman and Sardinian strain of my mother's family, mingled and died out in my veins."

On both sides Vigny came of good stock, less important perhaps than he imagined, but still ancient and respected. A certain François de Vigny had been

ALFRED DE VIGNY IN 1815
From a Portrait in the Musée Carnavelet
attributed to his Mother

ennobled by Charles IX in 1569. His mother's family, the Baraudins, who were incidentally of Piedmontese and not of Roman or Sardinian origin, had been admitted to the aristocracy by Charles III, Duke of Savoy, and the title had been confirmed by Francis V in 1543. The Baraudins followed the sea while the Vignys regularly went into the army, but no ancestor of either side appears to have won any great distinction. One of the Vignys, who happened to be governor of Brest at the time, had received a letter from Charles II, king of England, thanking him for his kindness to English royalists in exile. The Marquis Didier de Baraudin, Vigny's grandfather, had been a 'chef d'escadre' under Louis XVI. His grandfather's cousin, Louis Antoine de Bougainville, is one of the great names in the French navy. That was as near to fame as any of the ancestors had come. For the most part, following the usual custom of the noblesse de province, they retired from the army or navy after winning the croix de St. Louis and spent the rest of their lives on their estates hunting wolves and wild boar.

Galants guerriers sur terre et sur mer, se montrèrent
Gens d'honneur en tout temps comme en tous lieux,
    cherchant
De la Chine au Pérou les Anglais, qu'ils brulèrent
Sur l'eau qu'ils écumaient de Levant au Couchant;
Puis, sur leur talon rouge, en quittant les batailles,
Parfumés et blessés revenaient à Versailles
Jaser à l'Oeil-de-Boeuf avant de voir leur champ.

Gallant they proved themselves on land and sea,
Hunting the English foe relentlessly
From China to Peru, whose ships they burned
Down to the water's edge. The waves they churned
From East to West. And then their battles o'er
Perfumed and wounded to Versailles once more
They came, before retiring to their own domain.

Apparently no Vigny and no Baraudin had ever been excited by literature. They were all exclusively men of action. Vigny's mother was the first of the family to dream of a different way of life. Not that she had much time for dreaming, but she had a definite theory about her son's education which included other interests besides hunting and fighting.

Mlle. Marie Jeanne Amélie de Baraudin had been married at Loches in 1790 to a man twenty years older than herself. Eighteen months after marriage the Comte de Vigny, long an invalid, became a helpless cripple. From then on she was the mainstay of the family. Monsieur de Vigny, intelligent enough to realize his wife's greater intelligence, never interfered with her direction of affairs. The birth of Alfred on March 27, 1797, can hardly have been an occasion for great rejoicing. The Revolution had weighed heavily upon the family. Three sons had already been born in rapid succession, but they were sickly children and none of them had lived beyond infancy. Would it be possible to rear this last child? Monsieur de Vigny was sixty and his wife forty years old. If Alfred should not survive it looked as if the family must die out.

The sheer business of living during those terrible years of the Revolution and the Directory required no little resiliency, especially if one had the misfortune to be an aristocrat. Madame de Vigny's father, the former 'chef d'escadre,' was imprisoned. An émigré brother had been wounded and captured in the ill-fated expedition to Quiberon, and subsequently shot. Three of Monsieur de Vigny's brothers were serving in the army of the Prince de Condé. After the disbanding of Condé's army one of them, who had been a brigadier in the royal artillery, became a Trappist, and the other two were closely watched by the police. The Vigny family were therefore thoroughly suspect, and accordingly they were honored by the closest attention of the Comité de Surveillance.

As soon as they could get permission from the authorities the Vignys shook the dust of Loches off their feet and went to live in Paris. Hounded by the hatred in which all aristocrats were held they must have been delighted to start life over again in a new environment, surrounded by people of their own kind equally anxious to forget the nightmare years of the Revolution. They rented an apartment in the Elysée Bourbon, now the residence of the president of the French Republic, but at that time the home of a certain Citoyen Hovyn, 'entrepreneur de fêtes et de plaisirs publics.' Hovyn had divided the building into fifteen apartments and had transformed the garden, which stretched across what is now the Champs Elysées down to the Seine, into an amusement park. The Elysée had previously belonged to the Duchesse de Bourbon, mother of the ill-starred Duc d'Enghien. She had hoped to weather the storm of the Revolution by styling herself, in good republican fashion, 'Citoyenne Vérité.' Although her husband and brother were both émigrés she was allowed to live in one corner of the building until the Directory came into power. In 1798 the Elysée was sold as belonging to the nation and bought by speculators of whom Hovyn was the prime mover. On his death Mlle. Hovyn let the contract for the amusement park to Vellone, one of the many Italians who came to Paris in the wake of Napoleon's armies and became a restaurateur. Finally, in the year 1805, Napoleon decided that the Elysée would make a suitable palace for his brother-in-law, Joachim Murat, and the Vignys moved to a house in the rue Marché d'Aguesseau.

For their first six years in Paris the Vignys' home in the converted palace cost them 700 francs a year, not an exorbitant sum, but it was almost more than they could afford. The property of Madame de Vigny had been sequestrated, and her husband's small pension as a wounded captain had lapsed. They were forced to live on what she had economized from her dowry. The other apartments in the building were occupied by duchesses, destitute generals, jacobins, retired cooks and valets de chambre of the royal family.

Such was the world that unfolded itself to the enquiring eyes of Alfred de Vigny. Not that he was allowed to spend too much of his time listening to the entrancing conversation of this heterogeneous society.

Occasionally his father would take him to call on some remnant of the aristocracy in the Faubourg St. Honoré, but it was Madame de Vigny who planned the boy's education. Using 'Emile' as her text-book — Madame de Vigny was a great admirer of Rousseau — she showed her usual sound intelligence by giving her son a vigorous physical training. Cold baths, fencing and gymnastic lessons in the open air, were an essential part of the scheme. She also took him to the Louvre where he admired Napoleon's latest acquisition, the Apollo Belvidere. A piano teacher introduced him to the world of Mozart, Beethoven, and Cherubini. The delicate baby soon developed into a healthy boy with a wider range of interests than boys in the Vigny family usually possessed. If it was not in his mother's power to make him actually robust, by her sensible bringing up she saved him at least from the life of an invalid.

At the age of nine he was sent as a day boarder to the Pension Hix, a school patronized by the rich bourgeoisie and the more well-to-do officers of the Grande Armée. One of the few friends he made there was the son of a General D'Orsay, an exceptionally attractive boy whom he was to meet years later at Lady Blessington's. The Pension Hix may have satisfied the sons of the Napoleonic 'nouveaux riches' but it made young Alfred de Vigny acutely miserable. Forty years later he could still recall the dirty glasses of Seine water they were given for tea, and the eager delight with which he slammed the 'porte cochère' at the end of the day's work. Above all he remembered the bullying he was subjected to on account of his aristocratic manners. " At school I was persecuted by my companions; sometimes they would say to me: you have a ' de ' in front of your name; are you an aristocrat? I replied: yes, I am. Then they would set upon me. I felt that I belonged to an accursed race, and that made me sombre and pensive."

What an unjust world it was. His father and mother had taken special pains to prevent questions of rank assuming too great an importance in his eyes. Once when he had asked his father the meaning of the words 'noblesse' and 'mésalliance' the old gentleman had taken a pinch of snuff and blown it into the air. Those words, he had explained, had no more significance than these grains of snuff. His mother had pointed the explanation still more vividly. She had made him sit next to her at the piano, and she had sung an old song which Monsieur de Coulanges had composed for Madame de Sévigné after an argument over the age of a certain family:

Nous fûmes tous laboureurs, nous avons tous conduit notre charrue
L'un a dételé le matin, l'autre l'après-dinée.
Voilà toute la différence.

The aristocracy had stopped working sooner than other people. That was the only difference. It was characteristic of Monsieur and Madame de Vigny that they should have been such ardent legitimists and at the same time so sceptical of social distinctions. Obviously they had also actually lived through the appalling experiment of a kingless state. Years afterward Alfred de Vigny was only reflecting the teaching of his mother and father when he demanded that a man to please him should possess the mental outlook of a republican blended with the language and the manners of a courtier. He found his ideal in the character of Alceste, an Alceste incidentally that Molière would hardly have recognized, a splendid Prometheus of a man who bore no resemblance to the crotchety lover of Célimène.

Meanwhile the gilded youths of the Imperial noblesse were jeering at him for being an aristocrat. It was no unusual thing then any more than it is now for a talented boy to be unhappy at school, but to be jeered at for being a noble without ever tasting any of the privileges that nobility is supposed to confer —that was hard indeed. The English public school has long been the target for bitter criticism but it is not only in England that school life has been made intolerable for the sensitive boy. The lycée was just as much a nightmare to Lamartine, to Victor Hugo, or to Alfred de Vigny, as Eton and Harrow were to Shelley and Byron. Lamartine assures us that the games of his companions saddened him and their faces repelled him, that the masters were gaolers, prejudiced as well as incompetent. His one idea was to escape from his hateful prison, and he would spend hours gazing through the school gates at the distant mountains of Beaujolais dreaming of the happiness and the liberty he had left behind. Victor Hugo was no less eloquent upon the horrors of school life. While

he was revelling in his gay, careless existence in the
garden at the Feuillantines his mother was approached
by the principal of some grammar school and urged
to give her son a serious education. Victor congratulated himself that the choice between a dreary school
and a radiantly happy home was decided temporarily
at least in his favor. For Alfred de Vigny school was
made even more intolerable by the accident of his
aristocratic birth. All his life he was handicapped by
the consciousness of being born into one class of society and having to live as if he belonged to another.
His slight physique and his finely chiselled features
damned him irretrievably in the eyes of his companions. He did his lessons too easily, and he was
too good-looking. As a schoolboy, and later on as a
soldier and a poet, the curse of involuntary refinement
lay heavily upon him. He considered it his greatest
misfortune. " To make a literary reputation among
the masses," he notes in his journal, " one must be
repulsively ugly, dirty, pedantic, and vulgar." Perhaps
he had Balzac in mind when he wrote those words
— Balzac who could not talk without spluttering
through his jagged teeth, Balzac always greasy and
dirty, the idol of the bourgeoisie. It would be easy
enough to cite other instances, such as Victor Hugo,
where good looks proved a genuine literary asset, but
Vigny is probably not wrong in assuming that the
almost feminine refinement of his appearance, which
was completely belied by the resolute independence
of his character, militated against him in every walk
of life. His friend and commanding officer, Colonel

Fontanges, had the greatest difficulty in convincing a general inspecting his battalion that Captain Alfred de Vigny was a most efficient officer. In the army as at school sheer ugliness should have been less of a handicap than ethereal beauty.

After three years of unhappiness, if not actual misery, he was withdrawn from the Pension Hix and allowed to study at home. One of his teachers, an old abbé, had the happy idea of making him translate Homer into English and then compare his version with Pope's Iliad. In this way he acquired an admirable vocabulary of English though he always spoke it with an accent. Delivered from the tyranny of his contemporaries and the pedantry of schoolmasters he devoured one book after another. He started to write a history of the Fronde, he sketched out several comedies and tragedies, but always after going back to Corneille and Racine he tore them up in disgust. How impossible it was for any young man to devote himself whole-heartedly to the things of the spirit when the Napoleonic eagles were flying from Madrid to Moscow. The Vignys after all were not poets but men of action. Alfred decided on the artillery — mathematics interested him no less than literature — and he was sent to the Lycée Bonaparte to prepare for the Ecole Polytechnique. The idea of his son serving the monster who had assassinated the Duc d'Enghien must have been horrible to a good legitimist like Monsieur de Vigny, and yet what other career was there for a self-respecting young man but the army? Luckily Napoleon's abdication preserved his son from the disgrace of fighting under the tricolor.

On July 6, 1814, Alfred de Vigny was admitted to the Maison du Roi, an aristocratic corps consisting of four companies of Gendarmes Rouges. Only those were eligible for this corps d'élite who could prove their nobility. The Gendarmes Rouges involved a way of life far beyond Vigny's means. It was all very well to belong to the Maison du Roi if you were like young Alphonse de Lamartine whose mother lavished her fortune on his pleasures, but the Vigny family had no fortune to lavish. Alfred liked horses but he was not in a position to indulge his taste. Once again he felt the irony of belonging by birth to a society from which he was actually excluded by poverty. His family, who were hard put to it even to buy his uniform, had not chosen the Maison du Roi for snobbish reasons. As they said in a letter to the Minister of War, 'cet enfant a été élevé pour le Roi.' It was merely unfortunate that devotion to the king happened to be such an expensive luxury.

Upon the auspicious occasion of his becoming a Gendarme Rouge Monsieur and Madame de Vigny gave their son certain presents which they hoped would be useful to him. Monsieur de Vigny gave him an engraving of the arms of the family to be used for visiting cards. No doubt his new friends would be interested in heraldry. Madame de Vigny's gifts were of a more serious nature — the Imitation of Jesus Christ, the book in which he had learned to read, with the inscription "A Alfred son unique

amie," and a small Bible that had belonged to his
uncle, the Abbé Baraudin. The Bible was an unusual book for a Catholic to give to her son. How
great an influence it had upon him will appear later.
More touching than either of these gifts were the
'conseils à mon fils,' a code of life written out in
her own firm hand and calculated to guard him
against the world, the flesh, and the devil, if only he
would follow its precepts. Madame de Vigny showed
her eighteenth century upbringing by appealing more
to the reason than to the emotions. She impressed
upon him his duty to his King and his country, and
at the same time she warned him against intolerance
and against bitterness over the past. Certainly she
was a Royalist and a Catholic, but not an Ultra.
Above all, the burden of her instruction was self-
respect. The senses must be dominated by the will,
otherwise man would sink to the level of a brute.
Some of his brother officers might pride themselves
upon their debauchery, but she hoped that he would
remember the courtesy due to all women. By some
strange presentiment she warns him particularly
against actresses: "I hope you will never see them
except from the end of an opera glass, and that you
will never talk to them. Such women are incapable of
attracting a man of taste 'qui veut mettre de la
délicatesse dans ses liaisons.' What a characteristic appeal that was. A liaison without delicacy — what could
be more repulsive!

With this excellent equipment the young Gendarme du Roi clattered out of Paris behind the King's

coach. He had suddenly put away childish things. The mockery of his schoolmates at the Pension Hix dwindled into insignificance in his imagination, while his father's exploits in the Seven Years' War became more and more vivid. Fate had been kind to him after all. For a moment it seemed that he had been born too late, but now before his eighteenth birthday he had suddenly leapt into manhood. What did it matter if his brother officers teased him, asking him to lend them his razor, or if the peasant women along the route insisted on offering the adorable young mousquetaire bread and butter sandwiches. Of course he was young, but for the first time in his life he felt in tune with the times. Instead of perpetually feeding on the glories of the past he was actually making history himself. No young man can ever be happy unless he is in love with the present, and unless he is possessed by a great yearning for the future.

Madame de Vigny had made one mistake in his education — she had allowed him no companion of his own age. He had grown up in the society of older people. No boy can have been more steeped in the souvenirs, the dreams, and the disillusionment of the old aristocracy. It had not all been harmful by any means. Whatever the older generation can give — a consideration for others, an appreciation of the arts, a love of learning, and above all a most rigid sense of honor — they had given him abundantly, but they had always directed his gaze towards the past. It was high time that he should examine the strange new world in which he had to live.

ALFRED DE VIGNY

The death of his father in the year after Waterloo marks the end of Vigny's adolescence. The gallant old veteran, crippled for fifty years, had taught him an unobtrusive stoicism that he afterwards adapted to his own philosophy. " My child," he said to me, " I am not going to make any fine speeches but I feel that I am going to die. The old machine is running down. Make your mother happy and keep this with you always." It was the portrait of Madame de Vigny painted by her own hand. Vigny obeyed his father's instructions to the letter. Even when his mother's happiness demanded the surrender of his own, he never forgot those last words, " rends ta mère heureuse."

Much that his father had told him about the glory of war had to be painfully unlearned, but his father's courage in the face of poverty and physical suffering bit deep into his mind. It preserved him from the fallacy that so often disfigures romantic literature in every age and country — that man has some inherent right to happiness. It was the fallacy upon which Shelley wrecked his life. His steadfast refusal to accept the inevitability of evil has made him the patron saint of all idealists but for those of us who can not breathe the air of Utopia, who must live in ' the very world which is the world of all of us,' this battling against the universe ultimately degenerates into mere bravado. Nor is it true that the gallant souls in literature have invariably followed in Shelley's footsteps. The same spirit that animated Vigny, the aristocratic young officer in the king's bodyguard, crops out simultaneously in the letters of a young Cockney, but a Cockney with Shakespeare in his blood. "Young men for some time have an idea that such a thing as happiness is to be had, and therefore are extremely impatient under any unpleasant restraining. In time however, of such stuff is the world about them, they know better, and instead of striving from uneasiness, greet it as an habitual sensation, a pannier which is to weigh upon them through life." So wrote Keats in a letter to his publisher April 24, 1818. Like Vigny he learned at an early age that out of suffering there was no dignity, no greatness — that in the most abstracted pleasure there was no lasting happiness.

CHAPTER II

Ce n'était que cela, me dis-je, après avoir mis les épaulettes.

VIGNY

IT WAS NOT LONG BEFORE THE TINSEL OF ARMY LIFE
began to tarnish. After escorting the King into exile
the Compagnies Rouges were interned at Amiens
until after the Battle of Waterloo. Flight followed by
inactivity; such was Vigny's first and only experience
of active service. And when The Hundred Days was
over it must have been rather a shock to him to discover that the Maison du Roi was not popular. The
exclusiveness of this aristocratic corps and the exces-
sive elegance of its red and white uniform savored too
much of the ancien régime to please a populace that
was still wedded to the principles of the Revolution.
The veterans of the Grand Army could hardly be
expected to favor a regiment commanded by the
fledgelings of the old nobility. In September, 1815,
Louis XVIII, the only member of his family to sense
the drift of popular clamor, abolished the Maison
du Roi, and in the following year Lieut. Alfred de
Vigny was transferred to the Fifth regiment of the
Guard. For the next six years he did garrison duty
with his regiment in the vicinity of Paris, at Courbevoie, Versailles or Vincennes, and sometimes fur-

ther afield at Rouen or Nemours. The monotony of
army life soon began to tell on him. He found that he
had nothing in common with the other young officers
in the regiment, 'orators of the café and the billiard
table' as he calls them, men whose conversation was
invariably dull and usually disgusting. When they
were serious they discussed the minutiæ of their uniform but for the most part they idled away their life,
smoking and gambling.

It is no explanation of Vigny's disillusionment
to say that he was constitutionally unfitted for army
life. Even so great a soldier as Marshal Lyautey
was no less depressed by the drab sterility of garrison
duty in the provinces. We are probably justified in
assuming that Marshal Lyautey had more flair for his
profession than Alfred de Vigny, but until he exchanged a life of routine in a French depot for a life of
action in Madagascar or Morocco, Lyautey seems to
have felt, as did Vigny, that the army offered no
future to a young officer cursed with intellectual
curiosity and a passionate craving for a life of action.

More and more Vigny fell back on the society of
the older men, the captains who had risen from the
ranks, who had learned their trade in Egypt, in Italy
and in Russia. For their part, they were not sorry to
fight their battles over again with the serious young
lieutenant who showed such a proper respect for their
anecdotes. And yet, though he listened with rapt attention, his admiration was tempered by a half wistful criticism. He was beginning to feel the pathos as
well as the glory of army life: "In the evening we

would stroll through the fields and woods near the garrison, or along the sea-shore; the general look of the countryside or the slightest detail of terrain would give rise to inexhaustible recollections . . . and always these recollections were tinged with regret for the dangers of the past, with devotion for the memory of some great general, or with naive respect for some obscure hero whom they believed to be famous; through all these stories ran a vein of touching simplicity which filled my heart with veneration for the character of these old soldiers, forged in the flame of constant adversity."

How unsatisfactory their status was these childlike heroes hardly realized themselves. For twenty years they had been battling for liberty, so they were told, against all Europe, and now they were serving a Bourbon king who had been thrust upon them by their enemies. A life of unquestioning obedience to their superior officer had unfitted them for any trade except war. Compared to the deadening routine of garrison duty at Vincennes the adventures of these prematurely old men seemed to be poetry itself, but what was the actual value of their sacrifice? Alfred de Vigny was puzzled. Could his father, could all his ancestors be wrong? Was war the only possible career for a man of honor, and if not why was he drilling recruits into a state of mental servitude, in which loyalty was the only virtue and the exercise of individual judgment the unpardonable sin?

Vigny felt the dangers of passive obedience so strongly that years later, when he came to write

'Servitude et Grandeur Militaires,' he developed
the idea of the degradation of discipline to its fur-
thest limits. 'Servitude et Grandeur Militaires' is
one of the books to which the war has given a new
lease of life. No modern pacifist propaganda so completely exposes the folly of war and the sterility of
army life, all the more pathetic because of its ineffectual virtues. 'Laurette,' the first of the three tales
in the book, is the story of an old 'chef de bataillon'
whom the author when escorting Louis XVIII into
exile overtook on the march. This old man was leading along the Lille road, on a day of pouring rain, a
tired mule drawing " a wooden cart covered over with
three hoops and a piece of black oil cloth. It looked
like a cradle slung on two wheels." He too was escorting the king into exile after which he was going to
rejoin his battalion and fight on the other side. The
Restoration of the Bourbons involved the army in the
most complicated problems in loyalty. He had begun
life at sea, and had been taken from the merchant
marine to command a brig of war, when the navy
like the army was left without officers by the emi-
gration. In 1797, under the government of the Directory, he was appointed to command the 'Marat,' and
he had sailed from Brest under sealed orders. The
only passengers were a young bride and groom. The
man had been condemned to death for writing scur-
rilous verses on the Directory, but the sentence had
been commuted to deportation to Cayenne. Along
with these prisoners, whom he was ordered to treat
with respect, the captain received a packet with three

red seals, 'the middle one of enormous size,' not to be opened until the vessel reached one degree north of the line. As he was nailing up this forbidding packet in a nook of his cabin, the prisoner entered holding by the hand his ravishing young bride. The young couple won the good-natured captain's heart. He had no family and no ties. He offered on arriving at Cayenne to settle there with his little savings and adopt them as his children. On reaching the prescribed latitude he broke the fatal seal and read the sentence of death and immediate execution. He had become devoted to his passengers in the course of the voyage, and he bore no affection for those dirty lawyers who had ordered the execution, but his sense of duty left him no loophole of escape. The captain explained his predicament to the victim who accepted his fate without argument. Military discipline prevailed and the captain did as he was commanded. "That moment had lasted for me to the present; as long as I live I shall drag it after me as a galley-slave drags his chain." Laurette became a hopeless imbecile. Since her family would have nothing to do with her the captain dedicated his life to her service and protection. Disgusted with the sea he exchanged into the army. The unhappy girl had been with him ever since in all his campaigns, even in the retreat from Russia, tended by him like a daughter. Vigny parted from the old officer at the frontier. Long afterwards he learnt that an eccentric 'chef de bataillon' who was always busying himself about a little cart containing a mad woman had perished at Waterloo. The unfortunate girl consigned to a madhouse had died in three days.

A typically false romantic story is the reader's first impression, but Vigny insists that the story is true, that it had been told him by his cousin, the great admiral de Bougainville. Every time that Vigny uses 'I' in this book he maintains that he is speaking the literal truth. Certainly the execution of political prisoners was no rare occurrence at this time, but whether every detail of the story be true or not it shows how far Vigny had travelled since the time when he had thrilled over the bulletins of the Grand Army in the dim schoolrooms of the Pension Hix.

'La Veillée de Vincennes,' the next story in 'Servitude et Grandeur Militaires,' reveals what would at first appear to be the attractive side of discipline. The story itself is a charming idyll of army life but the moral illustrates Vigny's characteristically wistful bitterness. It deals with the life and destiny of an old adjutant of artillery whose acquaintance Vigny, an officer in the guards then in garrison at Vincennes, had made in the courtyard of the fortress on the eve of a general inspection. The adjutant was one of those Puritans of honor who can never satisfy himself that he has done his duty. Feeling that he would be eternally disgraced if the slightest inaccuracy were found in his report, he was counting over his shells and his barrels of powder for the hundredth time. Satisfied at last that his figures are correct he abruptly turns to humbler pursuits and produces a handful of hempseed for the 'belle poule' that is bringing up her twelve chickens under an old bronze cannon. Nothing could be more charming than the picture Vigny draws of the simplicity and the conscientiousness of this kindly old soldier. Uncle Toby and Corporal Trim were not more childlike or more completely devoted to the army than Vigny's adjutant of artillery. He had been brought up by the curé of his village to be a music teacher when a chance remark of Marie Antoinette suddenly decided him to become a soldier. On one occasion when he was playing in the park at Montreuil with Pierrette, a child of his own age, two exquisite ladies suddenly descended upon them. The lady in pink walked straight up to Pierrette and turning to her companion, remarked: " What did I tell you, there is my milkmaid costume for Thursday." Then addressing Pierrette: " My child, you must give all these clothes just as they are, to the people who will call for them. I shall send you mine in exchange." Looking at Pierrette's playmate she continued: " There is a young man who is going to be a soldier and I shall marry you to him." The children were so delighted and so overcome with embarrassment that they could hardly answer. Thus it was that the curé's dreams were shattered, and the promising young musician became a soldier in the Royal Auvergne regiment. Marie Antoinette and her companion, the Princesse de Lamballe, kept their promise. The Queen gave Pierrette a good dowry and she and her young soldier lover were finally reunited.

After listening to the adjutant's story of his life, a life incidentally of complete self-effacement, Vigny began to ruminate about his own career. How much nobler was this old soldier's resignation and scrupulous honor than his own overweening ambitions. The adjutant's story had lasted far into the night. A few hours after leaving him Vigny was awakened by a deafening explosion. One of the powder magazines had exploded. Still nervous about the morning's inspection the adjutant had gone his rounds once more. While he was groping his way in the dark the barrels of powder were somehow ignited and he was blown to pieces. The following day Louis XVIII visited the fortress and distributed a few gold pieces among the survivors, but he quite forgot the adjutant's family. "As a rule," remarks Vigny with quiet bitterness, "princes pass by too quickly." It was significant that no one, not even Vigny himself, expressed the slightest feeling of sympathy; to do so would have been considered a confession of weakness. On the contrary the soldiers prided themselves upon their callousness. Vigny wishing to display his bravado makes a sketch of the corpse. One of the young soldiers remembering that the adjutant's silk cravat is still good removes it from the body. In this story discipline stultified the emotions just as in 'Laurette' it had paralyzed the intelligence.

Now that Vigny had outgrown his father's military philosophy he was torn between an admiration for the selflessness of the professional soldier and a loathing for that surrender of conscience which seems inseparable from army life. Garrison duty taught him that the army was a savage mistress, that it developed

devoted martyrs or idle profligates, but that it offered
no future to the poet or to the man of the world.
Fortunately the very isolation of army life which he
so deplored had its compensations: " My term of military service was a second education for me, a real education, the only one that brings out the essential
qualities of the soul. Thanks to the confinement of
regiments in fortresses my life was that of a young
Benedictine or a Levite, and the army became as far
as I was concerned a second lycée . . . discipline is
a gaoler that compels one to stay at home." Obviously
the elegant young lieutenant who preferred poetry
and philosophy to gambling and drinking had missed
his calling. Perhaps it was not too late to change.

His father without being an intellectual man had
transmitted to him a natural unaffected taste for the
classics, while from his mother he had inherited
among other things a love of philosophy, of algebra,
and of geometry. Paul Valéry has shown us that poetry
and mathematics far from being incompatible are
really complementary to each other. It may be that
Madame de Vigny's taste for geometry was largely
responsible for the intellectual texture of his verse.
Certainly she was severely critical of ' Héléna,' his first
attempt to scale the heights of Parnassus. The margins
of her copy of this poem are filled with caustic comments — ' incompréhensible . . . C'est à refaire car
on écrit français pour les français.' ' Héléna ' is a semi-
Byronic effusion in which the heroine after being vio-
lated by the Turks narrates the incident at considerable length to her fiancé, and then commits suicide.

Vigny profited by his mother's criticism and never republished the poem. To the casual reader it is interesting only as showing how completely the young poet was dominated by Byron and André Chénier.

'Moïse,' the first of his great poems, written curiously enough at about the same time as 'Héléna,' in 1822, shows a very different influence. Here for the first time Vigny fell under the spell of the Old Testament. The Bible his mother gave him had become his constant companion. English poetry has always refreshed itself from the Bible, but Alfred de Vigny is the first French poet, if we except the Racine of Athalie and Esther, to be attracted by Biblical themes. Vigny read the Old Testament not merely as an introduction to Christ's teaching but as a treasury of Oriental culture. At the same time he read into the character of Moses one of his own most deeply cherished convictions — the loneliness of genius. Moses the appointed of God, the judge, captain and hierarch of the chosen race, cries to God in anguish of spirit for deliverance and rest, that the weariness and solitariness of heart of him who is lifted up altogether above his brethren be no longer imposed upon him, that the Almighty withdraw his gifts and suffer him to sleep the sleep of common humanity.

Ma main laisse l'effroi sur la main qu'elle touche,
L'orage est dans ma voix, l'éclair est sur ma bouche;
Aussi, loin de m'aimer, voilà qu'ils tremblent tous,
Et, quand j'ouvre les bras, on tombe à mes genoux,

ALFRED DE VIGNY

O Seigneur! j'ai vécu puissant et solitaire,
Laissez-moi m'endormir du sommeil de la terre!

The hand I touch quivers with helpless dread,
The storm is in my voice, the lightning round my
    head;
They love me not, behold them trembling all,
When I draw near, down on their knees they fall.
In lonely grandeur, Lord, my life I've passed,
O let me die like other men at last!

The idea that genius is incompatible with happiness,
that the artist is always lonely and misunderstood, is
one of the constantly recurrent themes in Vigny's
prose as well as in his poetry. It is the mainspring of
'Chatterton' and 'Stello,' of 'Moïse' and 'Le Mont
des Oliviers.' Translated into his own life it developed
that natural tendency to reserve that was so aston-
ishing to Dumas and so irritating to Sainte-Beuve.
    Moses arguing with God, pleading to be relieved
of the aura of greatness, is a very different hero from
the innumerable Childe Harolds and Renés of romantic literature. In Vigny the love of solitude developed a sense of pity, whereas in most of the literature of the period it developed only a more or less
petulant contempt for the rest of humanity. The note
of pity is still more evident in 'Eloa,' the strange story
of an angel born of a tear shed by Christ, a poem
which Théophile Gautier describes as 'the most beautiful, the most perfect perhaps in the French language.' Eloa, unlike the other angels, is attracted to

Satan. Her downfall is the result of her own goodness. She should have known that certain beings are outside humanity and below it, just as she is outside humanity and above it. Satan knowing that pity leads to sympathy and sympathy to carnal love, succeeds in dragging his unhappy mistress to the depths of Hell.

In spite of many exquisite passages the poem is definitely dated. It may be that pity is no longer a theme to conjure with. The twentieth century can stomach almost anything more easily than an unsophisticated angel. Guileless innocence for better or worse has become one of the stock figures of comedy. At the same time it must be admitted that ' Eloa ' has had a great influence upon French poetry. Without Vigny's example it is doubtful whether Lamartine and Victor Hugo would ever have written ' La Chute d'un Ange ' or ' La Fin du Satan.' Furthermore there are certain lines in ' Eloa,' such as

Triste amour du pêché! sombres désirs du mal!

and

Je suis le Roi secret des secrètes amours.

which point straight towards ' Les Fleurs du Mal.' As a matter of fact, Baudelaire was one of Vigny's warmest admirers, and the admiration was fully reciprocated. When Baudelaire was trying to storm the Academy, Vigny was one of the very few immortals who recognized his genius. ' You are a new proof,' Baudelaire writes to him, ' that a great talent implies always nobility of character and a most exquisite indulgence.'

ALFRED DE VIGNY

Among the more enthusiastic reviews of ' Eloa ' was an article in *La Muse Française* by a young man named Victor Hugo. *La Muse Française* was a vivid little review, primarily royalist and catholic, but young enough and romantic enough to question the omniscience of the Academy. Unfortunately it only ran for one year as the editor, Alexandre Soumet, suddenly decided that he would like to be in the Academy himself, an ambition which necessitated the abrupt termination of his review. The last number containing eulogies of Byron by Vigny and Hugo appeared in June 1824. While Vigny was still in the 5th regiment of the guard these two had become close friends. In spite of his complaints that the regiment was a monastery entirely cut off from the rest of the nation, Vigny seems to have been successful in escaping from his cell pretty frequently and enjoying the social life of Paris. Vigny was the older of the two but Hugo had been the first to appear in print. His fervently royalist odes on the birth of the Duc de Bordeaux and the death of the Duc de Berry had excited Vigny's warmest congratulations. A letter from Hugo dated October 31, 1820, indicates that they had already been friends for some time: " Adieu, *mon ami;* I use the words (*mon ami*) deliberately and I hope that henceforth they will be the only suitable description of our relationship." The generation of 1830 always assumed that friendships and liaisons could only be terminated by death.

Vigny and Victor Hugo had been introduced to each other by Emile Deschamps, the son of an old friend of Vigny's father. Emile Deschamps had a small post in the Administration de Finances, but at heart he was a poet. He was one of those invaluable spirits who without producing great poetry themselves are gifted with a talent for friendship and literary enthusiasm that makes them a great stimulus to others. Lamartine called him ' the salt and yeast of our sad time.' The group of young romantic poets known as the Cénacle used to meet in the salon of Emile's father, M. Jacques Deschamps. It included among others, Soumet, Victor Hugo, Vigny, Emile and his brother Antoni, with both of whom Vigny was on such intimate terms that Monsieur Deschamps treated him as his own son. The friendship between Vigny and the Deschamps family, unlike many of the friendships of the romantic era, lasted fifty years and was only terminated by death. Vigny and Victor Hugo were immediately drawn to each other, though in the long run their friendship was not to prove so enduring. Hugo was altogether too dominating and too egoistic a character to keep a friendship unsullied for fifty years. In the eighteen-twenties, however, there was no two young men more devoted to each other or more convinced of each other's genius than Vigny and Victor Hugo. Victor confided to his friend his apparently hopeless passion for the beautiful Adèle Foucher, and it was Vigny and Alexandre Soumet who signed the registry when they were married.

When Vigny was in garrison at Courbevoie he saw a great deal of his literary friends. On one occasion he brought Hugo and Emile Deschamps out to lunch

with the officers, and during the entire drive from
Paris to Courbevoie they talked in verse to the complete bewilderment of the coachman. Obviously the
young lieutenant de la garde was more at home with
Deschamps or Hugo than with his fellow officers. But
the precious hours of leave which he snatched from
the wearisome round of reviews and exercises were
not always devoted to literature. The salons of the
Faubourg St. Germain claimed at least some of his
attention. There were not many officers of the Garde
Royale, and there were certainly no poets in the Cénacle, whom the Princesse de Ligne or the Duchesse
de Maillé were so anxious to welcome to their parties.
Alfred de Vigny found his way quite naturally into
very different worlds. The Faubourg and the rising
school of romantic poets were both equally attracted
by the distinguished looking young officer who contrived to unite the poet, the soldier, and the gentleman, in one person. And yet, in spite of this apparently irresistible combination, Vigny was too
impersonal and too distant in his manner to excite
any passion more lively than curiosity and admiration. The impression that he made as a young man
can be pretty accurately gathered from the Mémoires
of Alexandre Dumas, one of the most worldly but
entertaining chroniclers of the period.

" Alfred de Vigny was a peculiar man; he was po-
lite, affable, gentle in all his dealings, but he affected
the most complete unworldliness — an affectation
that accorded perfectly with his charming appearance.
His well-chiselled, sensitive features were framed in

curly gold hair-making him look like a brother of the cherubim. Vigny never touched the earth except by necessity. When he did fold his wings and alight by chance on the summit of a mountain, one felt that he was making a concession to humanity. What particularly astounded Hugo and me was that Vigny never seemed to feel in any degree the coarse demands of nature, which some people, Hugo and I among them, satisfied not only without shame but with a certain sensuality. None of us had ever discovered Vigny in the act of eating. Dorval, who for seven years of her life passed several hours a day in his company, confessed to us with an astonishment amounting almost to terror that she had never seen him eat anything except one radish . . . All of which did not prevent Vigny from being an agreeable companion, a gentleman to the tips of his fingers, always ready to do you a service and quite incapable of doing you an injury."

Not the least of Vigny's services was the revision with Hugo's help of some hundred verses of Dumas' play 'Christine.' The first night had been pretty successful but there were certain feeble lines which the audience booed. While Dumas entertained his friends at supper Vigny and Hugo retired to another room with the manuscript and spent four hours revising the text. The incident throws some light on Dumas' happy-go-lucky methods of playwriting but evidently Vigny and Hugo did their repairs satisfactorily for on the next night the actors negotiated the weak spots without disaster.

One had to be a poet rather than a literary Jack of all trades like Dumas to understand Alfred de Vigny, and naturally enough it was a poet who first fell in love with him. Delphine Gay was not only a poet, but she was what was known in the literary world of the day as a Muse. A Muse was a young lady who wrote poetry and recited it in salons. The number of muses in Paris during the reign of Louis Philippe was estimated at nine thousand, which shows how the salons had changed since the days of Madame du Deffand and Mlle. de l'Espinasse. The ancien régime enjoyed talk above everything else. Talleyrand insisted that conversation was the greatest pleasure known to man, but the salons of the Restoration and the July monarchy, though they enjoyed conversation, demanded other things as well. They wanted to hear music, and, still more strange, they wanted to hear their friends recite poetry. So keen was the demand that a man might wend his way from salon to salon on the same evening and hear one ravishing creature after another recite the ' Lac ' by Lamartine or the inevitable sonnet by Félix Arvers. Delphine Gay was the most famous of all the Muses. Her mother, an author herself and a celebrated hostess under the Directory, had dedicated her to the life of the salon. She was extraordinarily beautiful; Gautier speaks of her ' bellezza folgorante ' to which Charles X himself had fallen a victim, but the attentions of an obscure young lieutenant in the Garde Royale excited her far more than the possibility of becoming another Madame de Maintenon. What a perfect match she and Alfred de Vigny would have made. Cynics might have smiled at their youth, their incredible distinction and their earnest enthusiasms, but the salons would have been at their feet. They met and courted at Nodier's receptions at the Arsenal, where Hugo and Lamartine read their verses, and in the more fashionable salons of the Duchesse de Duras and Madame d'Ancelot. Delphine wrote a charming poem, " Qu'il est doux d'être belle alors qu'on est aimée," which she doubtless recited on occasions when Vigny was present, but nothing happened. The romance budded and then withered without blossoming. Madame de Vigny disapproved of the match. Sophia Gay maintained that Madame de Vigny demanded a more aristocratic match for her son, but it was probably the lack of dowry rather than humble birth that inspired her objections to the match. She remembered too well her own struggles against poverty to be willing to accept a penniless daughter-in-law however talented and beautiful. A young officer with nothing but his pay to live on was hardly in a position, according to Madame de Vigny's philosophy, to marry for love. Vigny remembered his father's last words — " rends ta mère heureuse." Marriage with Delphine would have made his mother decidedly unhappy. As a soldier he had already experienced the bitter pleasures of renunciation. Military glory he had already been denied by being born too late; now his sense of duty compelled him to forego the chance of married happiness. In a letter to Victor Hugo he speaks of his ' misères du coeur,' but except for that one confession he accepted his mother's wishes without a murmur. Possibly she was right after all. Delphine Gay had one fault which even her admirers admitted. She laughed too easily. The romantic poets, like Lord Chesterfield, did not believe in open laughter, at least as far as young ladies were concerned. It was all very well for Gargantua to hold his sides, but an Olympian smile was as far as a decorous young muse should go. Madame de Vigny may have foreseen that her son could never be happy with a wife who giggled. Twenty-five years later when Delphine Gay was Madame de Girardin, Vigny wrote her a charming poem comparing her present fragile loveliness with the more obvious but less alluring beauty of her youth. As the wife of a successful journalist Delphine enjoyed a popularity she might never have known as the wife of an ethereal poet. Her death, in 1855, commemorated by Lamartine and Victor Hugo, was the signal for national mourning. Vigny himself never tasted such adulation.

The fleeting romance cut short by Madame de Vigny was soon forgotten in the excitement of the Spanish campaign. In the year 1823 it looked as if Vigny were to enjoy the long awaited experience of active service. The Congress of Verona had authorized the government of Louis XVIII to invade Spain with an army of a hundred thousand men to quell the popular uprising, and restore Ferdinand VII to the throne. At last the young gallants of the Restoration were to be given a chance to prove that bravery was not the exclusive virtue of the Napoleonic veterans. After nine years of garrison duty Vigny had been promoted cap-

tain and transferred at his own request to the 55th
regiment, which was to form part of the expedition-
ary force. He joined the regiment at Strasbourg in
March 1823, and within six weeks he was en route
for the Spanish frontier. The march across France
gave him the opportunity of stopping to see his aunt
the chanoinesse de Baraudin at Maine Giraud, a small
property near Angoulême. " Never have I seen anybody," wrote Vigny, " who lived more completely in
the past." She made him read the letter of his uncle
Louis de Baraudin, written to his relations near Quiberon on the eve of his death. More than ever did he
dream of a du Guesclin war, in which he might prove
himself worthy of his ancestors. He confided the unfinished manuscript of ' Eloa ' to Victor Hugo to be
published just as it stood in the event of his being
killed. How splendid it was to be writing casu-
ally about death in battle to one's literary friends.
The war with Spain turned out to be one of those delightfully informal wars that the modern world has
forgotten how to wage. It offered a maximum of variety and adventure with a minimum of bloodshed.
One of his friends, France d'Houdetot, a grandson
of Jean Jacques Rousseau, wrote him the most tan-
talizing accounts of the campaign from the siege of
Saragossa. Life was so gay and the Spanish women
were so charming; he positively must get there before
it was all over. But it was not to be. Fate steadily refused him the war for which he longed.

Vigny's ill luck pursued him, and his battalion
never crossed the Pyrenees. They were stationed at

Bordeaux, at Bayonne, at Pau, and they even gazed upon the promised land from the frontier fort of Urdos, but as Vigny had already discovered there was no panache in garrison duty. On the contrary, garrison life at Pau proved more than usually unpleasant. The 55th regiment was ardently Catholic and royalist while the Béarnais and particularly the townspeople of Pau were noted for their extreme liberalism. On one occasion the crowd attacked the officers. Nothing came of it and the incident was quickly forgotten by everyone except Vigny who brooded over this manifestation of popular ill-will. It was all very well for the 'Mémorial Béarnais' to proclaim the affection of the inhabitants of Pau for 'the adored family of our kings.' The fact remained that the army was the symbol of the king's authority, and that the army was unpopular. Vigny convinced himself that it was unpopular because it was cut off from the main stream of national life. Politically speaking soldiers were mere infants. They were incapable of holding any opinion on the issues of the day since they were alienated from the civilian population and trained to rely implicitly upon their officers. For a long time Vigny had hugged the delusion that with the declaration of war the cloud of inactivity that so oppressed him would automatically roll away, but the war had passed him by leaving him to guard the frontier. More than ever he felt himself shut up in a wooden horse that would never open in any Troy.

Poets are sometimes accused of sacrificing action to the facile charm of reverie, of being in fact ineffectual angels, but Vigny was never a dreamer by choice. He longed for a life of action and it was only because action was denied him that he took refuge in a world of ideas. A nature poet would have found consolation in the lovely countryside of the Pyrenees, but Vigny was no Wordsworth. Rapt contemplation of the mountain torrents of the Pyrenees was a poor substitute for the intellectual activity he craved. Instead of gaining new strength from contact with Nature he was depressed by it. ' Dieu! que le son du Cor est triste au fond des bois.' There is no more wistful poem than ' Le Cor ' in the whole range of romantic literature but it is utterly removed from the tender pantheism of the Nature poet.

Disillusioned with the army in which he saw no hope of advancement and cut off from his literary friends in Paris, Alfred de Vigny was thrust entirely upon his own resources. " My Bible and a few English pictures follow me like household gods. I pass from the sword to the pen here as everywhere else. I know nothing of Paris . . ." In spite of the slightly querulous tone of this letter, life at Pau had its compensations. Vigny made friends with the English colony which even then had established itself at Pau. " I am surrounded by English families," he writes to Victor Hugo, " and I ride in the mountains with these blond Ossian like people. If you only knew how poetic the English really are; how they revere genius and how obvious it is to them that genius is just as worthy of respect as monarchy. Every day I wonder why I have not known them better."

A rather unusual eulogy of the English character but the explanation is not far to seek. Among the English colony was a certain Sir Hugh Mills Bunbury, a typically rich eccentric John Bull, who had made a fortune in the West Indies and who now travelled about Europe in a specially devised carriage equipped with a bedroom and a dining-room. This strange milord had a daughter, Lydia, with whom Vigny promptly fell in love. " Douce et bonne comme une fille d'Otaïti," he describes her in a letter to Victor Hugo. Not a stimulating companion perhaps, certainly not as brilliant as Delphine Gay, but none the less very appealing to a young officer who was leading a life of enforced inactivity in a milieu that was entirely unsympathetic to him. Lydia's artlessness and her blond beauty more than compensated for her intellectual deficiencies. Then too she was English and there was something in the Anglo-Saxon temperament that always attracted Alfred de Vigny. Occasionally he might complain that the English were lacking in gaiety, but Vigny was not a gay person himself and the characteristic reserve of the Englishman, which foreigners are so apt to mistake for superciliousness, was a quality that Vigny particularly admired. This time Madame de Vigny had no objections, or only such objections as could easily be waived. The Bunburys to be sure were foreigners and Protestants, but they were substantial people — the family included governors and secretaries of state — and incidentally Sir Hugh Mills Bunbury was enormously rich. He was already seventy years old and it was generally understood that a large part of the fortune that he had accumulated in Guiana would be left to his daughter Lydia. This detail may have meant nothing to the young lovers but it meant a great deal to Madame de Vigny. She gave her consent to the match and on February 8, 1825, Captain Alfred de Vigny and Lydia Jane Bunbury were married in the Protestant chapel at Pau. It is significant that none of Vigny's fellow officers signed the registry. Madame de Vigny herself could not be present owing to the difficulties of the journey, so the wedding was an exclusively English affair.

The only person who seems to have been opposed to the marriage was Lydia's father. He may not have disliked Vigny personally, but in the eyes of a successful nabob like Sir Hugh Mills Bunbury a poet, even if he happened to be a soldier, was hardly a person to be taken seriously. Some years later when he chanced to meet Lamartine in Florence he confided to him that his daughter had married a French poet, but he had forgotten which. Lamartine enumerated certain names and finally mentioned Vigny. "Yes," exclaimed Sir Hugh Mills, "that is the man, that is my son-in-law." He died in 1839 after disinheriting Lydia in favor of his children by a second marriage.

Vigny's marriage marks the end of his military career. Actually he did not get his discharge for another two years but an unsuccessful attempt to transfer to the ' gardes du corps à pied,' a more aristocratic corps than the 55th regiment, combined with a dangerous weakness in the lungs decided him to shake the dust of the army from off his feet. In later years he was fond of grumbling about the ingratitude of the Bourbons: "I paid with sixteen years of service their sixteen years of ingratitude." That was not quite accurate. He only served fourteen years in the army during which time he was constantly on leave. The director of personnel at the Ministry of War, who happened to be a distant cousin appears to have been extraordinarily generous with leaves of absence. The mere writing of 'Cinq Mars,' necessitating as it did the reading of some 300 volumes in the Bibliothèque Royale in Paris, while his regiment was still stationed in the Pyrenees, hardly suggests that the army exacted the last pound of flesh. 'Cinq Mars' was conceived at Oloron in 1824 but it was actually written in Paris in 1825 and published in 1826. Finally in March 1827, after being continuously on leave for over a year, Vigny requested his discharge stating as his reasons, weak health and urgent family affairs.

It was true that for much of his army life Vigny had been a sick man. He had no sooner joined the Compagnies rouges as a boy of sixteen than he broke a leg in a fall from his horse, from which he was still convalescing when he went back to his battalion to escort the king into exile. Shouting orders across the barrack square had proved too much for his lungs and he began spitting blood. "I marched from Amiens to Paris in the pouring rain spitting blood the whole way, and asking for milk at every cottage but never breathing a word about my sickness." Again, three months later, the same ominous symptoms appeared.

ALFRED DE VIGNY

" I kept on my feet," he notes in the journal, " thanks
to my youth and spirit; one has to keep going until
death. It is only when a man is dead that the regiment believes in his sickness. After his death people
will say: it seems that he really was sick after all."
This is not the complaint of a malingerer. A man like
Vigny does not keep a journal to justify himself in the
eyes of the world, but he was too sensitive not to rebel
in the privacy of his notebook against the stupid
callousness of the whole army system. His literary
friends, particularly Sainte-Beuve, were inclined to
mock the Anglo-Saxon severity of his manner, be-
lieving it to be a deliberate imitation of his wife's
compatriots. How little they understood the real
Alfred de Vigny. His stoicism was merely what the
psychologists of today would call a ' defense mechan-
ism.' As he expresses it — " the sombre severity of
my character was not inherent in me; it was given
me by life. It was a reaction against the harshness
with which I was treated." In other words it was
Nature's method of adapting him to a career for
which he was temperamentally unsuited. As soon
as he married into a family of means it was
obvious that the enthusiasm with which he was
greeted by the literary and the social world would
alienate him more and more from the army. The fact
that a young officer happens to be blest with literary
talent is no recommendation in the eyes of his su-
periors. As far as the Ministry of War was concerned
Vigny was merely one of a thousand young captains
who had been born just too late to profit by the Napo-

leonic wars. And yet though fate had refused him the military glory for which his soul yearned, Vigny's years in the army were not wasted by any means. He spoke out eloquently against the evils of discipline but this same discipline taught him something that his fellow romanticists never learned — that man must suffer in silence. Thanks to those depressing but fortifying years of army routine he acquired a mastery over himself, a capacity for dominating circumstances that later fashioned him into a great philosophic poet.

CHAPTER III

Quel ravissant coup d'oeil de cheminées! J'adore ces cheminées . . . Oh oui, la fumée de Paris m'est plus belle que les solitudes des bois et des montagnes.

VIGNY

THE PARIS IN WHICH THE YOUNG ALFRED DE VIGNYS settled was not perhaps more beautiful than the Paris of today but it was undeniably more intimate. The Madeleine, where they were remarried to satisfy the Catholic scruples of Vigny's mother, was on the extreme edge of the city. It had only just been built, and in the evenings the Parisians would foregather in the rue Royale to admire the moonlight on the facade much as the Athenians must have foregathered of an evening in front of the Acropolis. Already it had become the fashionable church, and the best families in Paris were sending their children there to be educated by the Abbé Dupanloup, who years later with the best intentions performed a doubtful service for the Faith in awakening the intelligence of young Ernest Renan. As yet there was no Avenue de l'Opéra and no boulevard St. Germain. Passy was still a charming village on the outskirts of Paris, the Arc de Triomphe still unfinished had been planted in a forest

clearing, and the Bois de Boulogne was in the depths
of the country. The bourgeois with sporting pro-
clivities could flush a covey of partridges in what is
now the Place Clichy, stop for a glass of milk on his
way home at one of the farms in Montmartre, and
be back in his shop on the Boulevards before the
fashionable world was awake. Across the river Musset was dreaming of poetry in the Luxembourg gardens, while in the rue Notre Dame des Champs
Sainte-Beuve was forming a temporarily delightful
but eventually disastrous intimacy with the Victor
Hugos. Mademoiselle Mars was still a favorite at the
Théâtre français; Madame Récamier and Chateaubriand were entertaining literature and aristocracy
at the Abbaye aux Bois — in heavily curtained rooms
for Madame Récamier is fifty years old and, alas, no
longer the beauty that she was, but her wit and kind-
lines are still as fresh as ever. The society of the first
Empire was flocking to the salon of Marshal Junot's
wife, the Duchesse d'Abrantès, who lived at No. 18
rue Rochechouart. Here, in addition to the Napoleonic generals that one was sure of meeting, might be
seen a clever young artist named Gavarni, whom the
duchess had just discovered. He was one of the few
friends who remained faithful to her long after she
had squandered her fortunes in reckless generosity.
Another popular hostess was Madame Vigée-Lebrun,
now eighty years old, whose portraits had so charmed
the court of Marie Antoinette. In spite of her age this
gallant old lady was still capable of fascinating her
guests by the verve of her conversation. She lived in

the rue St. Lazare, now in the heart of Paris but at that time a rather pleasant suburb.

The salons of Madame Récamier, the Duchesse d'Abrantès, and Mme. Vigée-Lebrun, and there were many others, reflected the spirit and the outlook of the older generation. Youth may have paid its respects to Chateaubriand and Madame Récamier, but if we want to see the young poets and artists of the day really enjoying themselves it is not at the Abbaye-aux-Bois that we should look for them. We shall be more likely to find them at the Arsenal, a gloomy old building dominating the river at the end of the Quai des Celestins. The Arsenal was not used as such any longer but as a library, and the librarian was one Charles Nodier whose evening receptions became the cradle of the romantic movement.

Charles Nodier was considerably older than Vigny or Victor Hugo. He had had the distinction of being arrested at Strasbourg in 1793 and of being brought before St. Just, who in a moment of unusual tenderness had released him from the clutches of the guillotine. Afterwards he had been attached to General Pichegru's headquarters but he was too absent minded for soldiering. He was always regarded even by his friends as an overgrown child. Heine insisted that when you had been guillotined several times in your youth like Charles Nodier it was only natural that you should have lost your head by the time you grew up. At one moment he had cherished a wild scheme of teaching political economy in Bessarabia but fortunately this fell through and in 1824 he found him-

self librarian of the Arsenal. At his celebrated receptions Nodier played the rôle of conciliator between
the romantics and the classicists. He was himself an
ardent romantic and at the same time an eighteenth
century man of letters. His was the only salon where
all shades of opinion, literary and political, were
tolerated. Under the reign of Louis Philippe the
charm of society was gone for people were afraid to
talk and each salon represented just one point of
view, but at Nodier's evening parties, even in 1830
when the monarchy was dying, discussion always was
friendly. One might meet a host of adversaries but
never an enemy. Good talk was not the only attrac-
tion at the Arsenal. Up until ten o'clock the evening
was devoted to conversation and the recitation of
poetry. From ten until one everybody danced, except
for those few like Lamartine who thought the waltz
'a lascivious dance.' Dumas has described the evenings at the Arsenal and the infinite charm of Charles
Nodier and his daughter Marie with his usual gusto.

After dinner the long lean figure of Nodier would
uncoil itself in front of the fireplace and he would embark upon his reminiscences. Out of his memory and
his imagination he would conjure up the most wonderful stories. It made no difference whether it were
a romance, a battle in La Vendée or a drama of the
Revolution. His audience was always spellbound and
the story always came to an end too soon. Why it
needed to end nobody ever knew for Nodier could
have gone on indefinitely drawing from the riches of
his imagination. "No one applauded," says Dumas,

" any more than one applauds the murmur of a brook, the song of a bird, or the perfume of a flower, but when the murmur is stopped, when the song dies away and the perfume evaporates, we listen and wait and yearn for more." But Nodier would slide gently into his arm chair: " Assez de prose, des vers, des vers, allons." Whereupon Hugo and Lamartine would take turns reciting their latest ode or elegy. The guests were invariably intoxicated by these mellifluous draughts of poetry. After the applause had died down Marie Nodier would go to the piano. That was the signal for the quadrille. Furniture was pushed aside and the dancers took their places. Nodier went to the card table but most of the guests preferred dancing or talking to the lovely daughter. Presumably Félix Arvers was one of those who crowded around the piano, the lovelorn Félix Arvers whose one passport to fame, the sonnet ' Mon âme a son secret, ma vie a sa mystère,' is supposed to have been inspired by Marie Nodier. At one o'clock Madame Nodier intimated that it was time for the guests to go home by threading her way through the crowded salon with the nuptial warming pan. Her husband followed her obediently to bed and the party was over.

Except for the talent of Charles Nodier and of his guests it was not a lavish entertainment. The refreshments consisted of ' eau sucrée,' orangeade and occasionally a ' sirop de groseilles,' but the best vintage wines could not have produced more brilliant conversation or more genuine joie de vivre. ' In the army of the romantics,' says Gautier, ' every one was young,' and incidentally everyone was also poor, but what an extraordinary array of talent there was packed into that little salon at the Arsenal. Within a few years Lamartine, Hugo, Dumas, Musset, Vigny, Sainte-Beuve, Delacroix and David d'Angers would go their separate ways but for the moment they were all held together by the social genius of Charles Nodier.

Alfred de Musset commemorated these evenings at the Arsenal years later in verses addressed to Charles Nodier that are not to be translated.

> *Ta muse, ami toute française,*
> *Fort à l'aise*
> *Me rend la soeur de la santé*
> *La gaieté.*

> *Elle rappelle à ma pensée*
> *Délaissée*
> *Les beaux jours et les courts instants*
> *Du bon temps*

> *Lorsque, rassemblés sous ton aile*
> *Paternelle,*
> *Echappés de nos pensions*
> *Nous dansions,*

> *Gais comme l'oiseau sur la branche*
> *Le dimanche*
> *Nous rendions parfois matinal*
> *L'Arsenal.*

ALFRED DE VIGNY

La tête coquette et fleurie
  De Marie
Brillait comme un bluet mêlé
  Dans le blé.

Tachés déjà par l'écritoire,
  Sur l'ivoire
Ses doigts legers allaient sautant
  Et chantant.

Quelqu'un récitait quelque chose,
  Vers ou prose,
Puis nous courions recommencer
  A danser.

Chacun de nous, futur grand homme,
  Ou tout comme,
Apprenait plus vite à t'aimer
  Qu'à rimer.

Alors dans la grande boutique
  Romantique,
Chacun avait, maître ou garçon,
  Sa chanson. . . .

Paris in 1826 was far from being the Mecca of ex-
patriates that it is today. It was a pleasant French
city of some 700,000 inhabitants. According to Mrs.
Trollope, an intelligent though not an infallible observer, ' every English person that comes to Paris is
absolutely obliged to speak French. If they shrink

[54]

from doing so they can have no hope of either speaking or being spoken to at all.' It is only fair to add that another, and a more aristocratic, traveller, Lady Morgan, gives us a very different impression. Lady Morgan, a vivacious Irish woman who adored Paris and all its works, was irritated by the all prevalent Anglomania. Apparently the Parisian shopkeeper insisted in 1829 as he does today upon airing his English. Tourists were beset at every turn with placards advertising hot mutton pies, oyster patties, Devonshire cider, spruce beer and London porter. Young Frenchmen assured her that 'everything English, except their politics, is now in Paris popular and is deemed romantic; and we have romantic tailors, milliners, pastry cooks and even doctors and apothecaries.'

Whether the current of Anglomania flowed from shopkeeping into society is more doubtful, but at any rate it was not powerful enough to make Madame Alfred de Vigny a force in her husband's career. Unlike Lamartine's wife, who was also an Englishwoman, she was quite incapable of enjoying, even as a spectator, the world of letters into which she had married. Miss Mary Ann Elisa Birch in becoming Madame de Lamartine became also a Catholic and a Frenchwoman, while Lydia Bunbury remained uncompromisingly Protestant and English. Whether she ever read his books no one ever knew, but certainly she never learned to speak French with any fluency. She traversed his life without penetrating into any of its recesses. At the same time Madame de Vigny was pathetically mid-Victorian in her helplessness. Without any of the charm of a Dora Copperfield she was equally dependent upon the ministrations of her husband. After the first two or three years of marriage she became a chronic invalid, and her radiant beauty evaporated. The lovely English girl whom Vigny had fallen in love with at Pau matured into a dull, massive woman who looked like a housekeeper without possessing any of the talents usually associated with that office. Even her own countrywomen complained that she was lacking in vitality. Henrietta Corkran, an English friend of the family, describes Madame de Vigny as a good-natured Mrs. Malaprop — kindly enough but essentially stupid. She would speak of some one as being as proud as Luther instead of Lucifer, and of her friends being excluded from an invitation when she meant included.

With this apparently unsympathetic woman Vigny lived happily for nearly forty years. He was not faithful to her, and she knew it, but his passionate liaison with Marie Dorval never interfered with his affection for his wife and his tender solicitude for her comfort. Sometimes he dreaded the possibility of his dying young and leaving her alone in the world, "a woman so timid, so easily frightened, so good and so naïvely innocent." Perhaps he luxuriated a little too much in the rôle of the devoted husband sacrificing himself to his sick wife, but no poet has ever played the part of a trained nurse so continuously as Alfred de Vigny. His wife and his mother in her old age were both helpless without him, and if in his journal he never allowed himself to forget how es-

sential he was to them, at least he never posed as a
martyr before the world. Whether he would have
been happy with a more lively intelligent woman is
very doubtful, for Vigny was not one of those men
who require a stimulus from the outside. He liked
Lydia's placid good nature, and her utter dependence
upon him flattered his vanity. She was not only his
wife but his child, and he took a mother's pleasure in
shielding her from the cruel world. The story that she
deliberately deceived him about her fortune, and that
she later confessed to him in her execrable French,
" je avais trompé vo parce que je aimai vo," may be
apocryphal but the very existence of such a story
proves her dog-like devotion. She loved him whole-
heartedly, and though she was never able to share any
of his intellectual interests they were none the less
satisfied with each other. In his curiously formal way
he felt at home with her as he never felt with other
women. Long after his passion for Marie Dorval had
burned itself out his relationship with Lydia remained as equable and impregnable as ever.

One virtue at least, a negative one but none the
less important in the wife of a poet, Madame de
Vigny did possess. She never obtruded herself and
she never claimed to be more intelligent than she
was. The only reference to Madame de Vigny that
is in any way complimentary comes from the pen
of Théodore de Banville. As a young man he had
been asked to a reception by Alfred de Vigny upon
whom he had left a copy of his first book of poems.
He was much impressed by the dignity of the occa-

sion — Madame de Vigny in beautiful lace, looking like a princess, very kind and affable, and Vigny himself dressed with English correctness treating everybody including his wife with a studied old world courtliness that might have seemed ridiculous in any one else but which was perfectly natural in him. "Each time that Madame de Vigny had to leave the salon for a moment to look after some domestic detail, for like all great ladies she was a good housekeeper (Vigny's intimate friends did not think so) the poet would offer her his hand and lead her to the door, as they do at Court. In the same way when she came back into the room he went up to her, bowed, and led her back ceremoniously to her chair. As fools were never invited to this house no one thought of being surprised at these manners or of finding them exaggerated."

At this time the Vignys were living in a modest second story apartment in the rue des Ecuries d'Artois, now No. 6 rue d'Artois. They had moved there in 1833 and it was there nearly thirty years later that they both died. Banville speaks of the beautiful pictures on the walls, of the antique furniture and of the grand piano made of some rare precious wood, but some allowance must be made for the ardent imagination of a young poet. Anatole France, another promising young author who at the very outset of his career enjoyed Vigny's hospitality, mentions a portrait of the poet Regnard, a terra cotta of the Virgin with outspread wings, a dreaming archangel sent to Vigny by an unknown admirer of 'Eloa,' and a

bust of Cinq Mars. English visitors were more inclined to notice the Spartan simplicity of the Vigny
salon, the dull red chintzes and the one table with
its paper bound books. Certainly a stranger coming
from the Hugos in the Place des Vosges, or the Lamar-
tines in the rue de l'Université would have been
struck by the absence of bric-a-brac and pseudo
Gothic ornamentation in the restrained salon of the
rue d'Artois.

It must soon have become apparent to Vigny's literary friends that Madame de Vigny might be ignored.
It was all very well for Victor Hugo to maintain in a
letter of congratulation to Vigny on his marriage —
" our wives will be as devoted to each other as we are "
— but it can only have taken a very few meetings to
convince Lydia de Vigny and Adèle Hugo that in
spite of Victor's warm-hearted enthusiasm the two
families could never be intimate. Madame de Vigny's
social life was limited to the small British colony at
Dieppe, where they spent their honeymoon, and the
Wednesday afternoons in the rue d'Artois. Possibly
they went to receptions at the British Embassy but
they can hardly have felt at home with Lord Gran-
ville the ambassador, the greatest gambler in Paris,
'the Wellington des joueurs' as the French called
him, who lost £23,000 at one sitting. That was not a
milieu in which either of them could shine to advantage. Paris must have seemed a friendless place
to Madame de Vigny. She was not fitted to cope with
the noisy vitality of Victor Hugo and his satellites,
nor can she have shown to much advantage in the

more aristocratic salons of the Restoration. Weak health combined with several miscarriages left her an invalid for life. " My dear Lydia, who has been ill for nearly a year," writes Vigny in 1826, " is at present rosy and happy, but alas there is no baby; that is my only sorrow, a temporary one I hope." Unfortunately it was not temporary. He had hoped to distinguish himself in war and when that satisfaction was denied him he longed for children to perpetuate his name and family. Fate which had so many cruel blows in store for him decided otherwise. In the meantime Lydia tended to shut herself up more and more in the little apartment in the rue d'Artois while Vigny, always in demand in the beau monde, made the rounds of the salons.

One of the salons where Vigny was always persona grata was Madame d'Agoult's. It was in this salon, ' improvisé dans une auberge,' according to George Sand, that one met the most brilliant people in every walk of life — Lamennais and Heine, Ingres, Chopin and Meyerbeer. Madame d'Agoult the mistress of Liszt, who was too busy with his concert tours to pay much attention to her, was one of the first hostesses to bridge the gap between the old aristocracy and the young lions of the romantic movement. It was there, as might be expected, that one heard the best music in Paris, the Symphonie Fantastique of Berlioz, Schubert's songs translated by Vigny's friend Emile Deschamps, and Chopin's Mazurkas. It was there too that Vigny had the terrible experience of reciting one of his poems, ' La Frégate,' to an utterly unsympathetic audience. Perhaps mere poetry was a dull thing to these music lovers, but Vigny accepted their chill silence imperturbably. "My frigate has been ship-wrecked in your salon," was all that he remarked to his hostess as he left the room. The silence was finally broken by an audible whisper from the Austrian Ambassador — "Ce monsieur — est-il un amateur?"

If Madame d'Agoult's friends did not appreciate his literary talent there were other people not less distinguished who did. Sir Walter Scott, who visited Paris in 1826 and who was fêted by everybody from the Royal family down to the market women of La Halle, was genuinely touched by Vigny's admiration. Col. Bunbury, Madame de Vigny's uncle, took him to call upon Sir Walter in his rooms at the Hotel Windsor. "One does not often meet great men these days," remarked Vigny upon being presented, "the only ones I have met are Bonaparte, Chateaubriand and yourself." Col. Bunbury interpreted, as Vigny had not yet learned to speak English fluently, and Scott replied appropriately. After a few moments' conversation about 'Cinq Mars' the visitors withdrew. Scott's rather ungenerous entry in his journal referring to this visit need not blind us to his respect for the author of 'Cinq Mars': "Cooper (i.e. Fenimore Cooper) came to breakfast, but we were 'obsédés' partout. Such a number of Frenchmen bounced in successively and exploded (I mean discharged) their compliments, that I could hardly find an opportunity to speak a word, or entertain Mr. Cooper at all." Like many other lions Scott found himself exhausted by

the attentions of his admirers, but he was not querulous by nature and he was not indifferent to success.
" I am ungracious," he admits, " not to be so entirely
thankful as I ought to be to this kind and generous
people." When he went back to Abbotsford he took
with him a copy of ' Cinq Mars ' inscribed to Sir Walter Scott, témoignage d'admiration, A. de Vigny.

The appearance of ' Cinq Mars ' marks the high
water mark of Scott's influence in France. As Victor
Hugo said, and he meant it as the highest kind of
compliment, ' there is no doubt that if this book had
been presented as a new novel by Walter Scott, translated by Charles Nodier, many a reader would have
been deceived.' Up to 1830 one million five hundred
thousand copies of Scott's novels are said to have been
sold in France alone. In view of this gigantic success
it is not surprising that in the salon of 1831 Heinrich
Heine counted over thirty pictures inspired by scenes
in the Waverley novels. The vogue spread through
all classes of society. Dressmakers and duchesses, artists and students were all devoured by a passion for
Sir Walter Scott. The Duchesse de Berri was in the
habit of giving fancy dress parties in which the guests
were requested to appear as heroes and heroines of
Scott's novels. In the year 1827, the year after his visit
to Paris, the theatres reverberated with the names of
Scott's heroes. There was one evening when the enthusiastic amateur of Waverley would have had to
take his choice between ' Louis XI at Péronne ' at the
Théâtre français, the ' Labyrinth of Woodstock ' at
the Odéon, and ' Leicester,' an adaptation from

Kenilworth by Scribe and Auger, at the Opéra
Comique.

But the most convincing and the most permanent
result of Scott's popularity is 'Cinq Mars' itself. Of all
the novels directly inspired by Waverley it is the only
one with the possible exception of Balzac's 'Les
Chouans' that is still readable. If we compare 'Cinq
Mars' with Quentin Durward the extent of Vigny's
debt is immediately apparent. The characters in the
two novels have more than a passing resemblance to
each other; Crawford and Bassompierre, Dunois and
de Thou, Tristran l'Hermite and Laubardemont,
Isabella de Croye and Marie de Gonzaga, are obviously hewn from the same quarry. The two heroes,
Cinq Mars and Quentin Durward, though one is
grave and the other gay, might well pass as brothers.
The difference between Scott and Vigny is that Vigny
relies on historical characters to bear the brunt of the
story, whereas Scott uses them only as a background
against which creatures of his own imagination enact
their drama. Vigny thought that Scott's method was
too easy, but in attempting to improve upon it he
was sometimes compelled to falsify history. Historians
have never been satisfied with Vigny's Machiavellian
Richelieu, and even Machiavelli would have hesi-
tated to make use of such a contemptible specimen of
human nature as Vigny's Père Joseph. Worse than
that Vigny thinks nothing of making Milton and
Descartes meet in Marion Delorme's salon when one
was in Italy at that moment and the other in Holland; or of having Milton recite pages from Paradise

ALFRED DE VIGNY

Lost some twenty years before a line of Paradise
Lost had been written. Modern readers are equally
bewildered by the extraordinary knowledge of the
future possessed by Vigny's characters. Bassompierre
and Bouillon predict the Revolution. Anne of Aus-
tria surveying the mutinous crowd from the balcony
of the Louvre suddenly fades away into Marie Antoinette. The novel ends with a discussion between
Corneille and Milton in which Corneille foresees a
monument to Desaix, the hero of Marengo, and Milton predicts the rise to power of an unknown man
named Oliver Cromwell. Of course Vigny committed
the artistic crime, so prevalent in the nineteenth century, of writing a novel with a purpose. He wishes to
prove that Richelieu destroyed the balance of power
between the king and the nobles, and thus paved the
way for the collapse of the monarchy. He was intent
on tracing a parallel between the nobility that surrounded Louis XIII and the aristocracy of his own
day. Both Louis XIII and the reigning sovereign,
Charles X, were deprived of the support that should
have rightly been theirs by Richelieu's policy of iso-
lating the monarchy from the rest of France. If
Charles X had had the advice of a vigorous aristocracy
instead of the blind obedience of a creature like Polignac he would never have lost touch with his people. Such would seem to be Vigny's thesis. Lady Morgan was only reflecting popular opinion when she
described this novel as the best course in practical
politics that can be presented.

Meanwhile the book floated to popularity in the

wake of the Waverley novels, and like the Waverley novels it quickly made its way abroad. Personalities as different as John Stuart Mill, Margaret Fuller, and Lady Blessington, delighted in this new Walter Scott of the Faubourg St. Germain. Three editions were called for before it was a year old, the last of the three being printed by young Honoré de Balzac, who was soon to give up his printing press and embark upon a more lucrative career. Victor Hugo, always downright in his enthusiasms, maintained that it was one of the most remarkable books of the epoch — ' the public will read it as romance, the poet as drama, and the statesman as history.' Amid all this chorus of approval there was one dissenting voice. The *Globe,* the leading periodical of the liberals, refused to be stampeded into admiration. Its review of ' Cinq Mars ' was anonymous. The author complained that the history was false, and that Vigny never succeeded in detaching himself from his characters. He admitted that there were certain poetical passages but even here his praise was guarded. The language seemed to him pretentious, or as some say ' romantic.' Later it leaked out that the article was by a Monsieur Sainte-Beuve who had recently come up to Paris from Boulogne to study medicine, and had gradually drifted into literature. He had made the acquaintance of the Victor Hugos through a complimentary and discriminating review of the ' Odes et Ballades.'

He was not an attractive young man, this Monsieur Sainte-Beuve, but his enthusiasm for poetry naturally endeared him to the Victor Hugos. This diffident, awkward, round-shouldered medical student, who knew nobody and who looked so obviously the bourgeois that he was, had somehow acquired a knowledge of literature and of literary criticism that was unbelievable. He was a poet himself too, but when Hugo called upon him to recite his verses he would beg the children to make a noise, which they very obligingly did, so that his recitation should not be heard. It was not long before his acquaintance with the Hugos ripened into intimacy. They discovered that they lived almost next door to each other in the rue Vaugirard, which made it delightfully easy for Monsieur Sainte-Beuve to drop in at all hours of the day. The tranquil sympathy of Adèle Hugo soon began to appeal to him even more than the full flood of Victor's genius, but for the moment there was no question of anything but literature between them. On his first visit Madame Hugo happened to ask him who it was that had written the unsympathetic review of 'Cinq Mars' that appeared in the *Globe*. Sainte-Beuve admitted that he was the culprit. It was an awkward confession to have to make to Vigny's warmest admirers, but luckily Victor Hugo was enough of an egotist to seize the opportunity for expounding his own literary theories. Sainte-Beuve listened entranced. A few days later he submitted some of his first ventures in poetry for Victor's consideration. The verdict must have been encouraging for from that day Sainte-Beuve dates his conversion to the romantic school. For the next three years Sainte-Beuve sat at the feet of the great Victor. He was one of the chosen band who attended the reading of 'Cromwell' in Madame Foucher's large drawing room at the Hotel des Conseils de Guerre. Perhaps he was not quite so impressed by that turgid drama as some of the other young lions of romance. He even suggested that it was too long—the playing of it would have taken about six hours if it had ever been produced—but Hugo was too impatient and too prolific to bother about rewriting. It is significant that Vigny was not present at the reading of 'Cromwell.' Hugo may have felt that it was too soon since that carping review in the *Globe* to attempt a meeting between his old friend and his new satellite. Not until the following year, 1828, did the ex-officer and the ex-medical student get to know each other. There was no reason to suppose that a fastidious gentleman like Alfred de Vigny should be attracted to the shifty-eyed, obsequious Sainte-Beuve—" pas laid, vilain," was Madame Hugo's description—but this young critic, unprepossessing as he was, had an extraordinary capacity for making himself liked. He immediately set to work to erase the impression of the unpleasant review. The man to whom Victor Hugo had dedicated his latest volume of poetry—'au bon ami Alfred, au grand poète de Vigny'—must certainly be worth cultivating. Hugo had initiated him to the beauties of 'Eloa' which he had at first been inclined to think too 'séraphique' and 'superfine.' To know Vigny was to know romanticism at its most exquisite. Once the awkward first meeting was over the acquaintance soon ripened into friendship. Within a year Sainte-Beuve was writing to him 'mon cher et excellent ami,' to thank him for the beautiful present he had sent him, a copy of the third edition of 'Cinq Mars,' and promising himself 'a day of delight' in re-reading it. Vigny must have been considerably molli-fied by such insinuating flattery but in case that were not enough he was offered a more direct apology in verse.

Et toi frappé d'abord d'un affront trop insigne
Chambre des saints amours, divin et chaste cygne,
   Qu'on ose rejeter,
Oh! ne dérobe plus ton cou blanc sous ton aile;
Reprends ton vol et plane à la voute eternelle
   Sans qu'on t'ait vu monter.

As poetry these lines may leave something to be desired but as an 'amende honorable' for previous discourtesy there is no fault to be found in them. Vigny was enchanted. "You are a poet," he replies, "who will never perish." It is true that the still small voice of the journal corrects this extravagant praise — "by sheer intelligence he has written excellent verses without being a poet at heart" — but no doubt he was pleased by Sainte-Beuve's eager friendliness. What-ever resentment he harbored had been melted by the warm sunshine of flattery.

One of the more innocent forms of mutual ad-miration practiced by the romantics was the reading of a play before a group of sympathetic friends. No sooner was the ink dry on his manuscript than an author would summon his intimates around him and declaim his masterpiece before them. On the tenth of July, 1829, Victor Hugo gave a reading of ' Marion Delorme.' Vigny followed a week later with his ' More de Venise.' They were both brilliant occasions. Such a display of talent as was gathered together to listen to these plays may possibly have been equalled at the Mermaid Tavern but assuredly nowhere else. Painting was represented by Eugene Delacroix, fresh from the studio of a young Englishman named Bonington. A striking figure was this Eugene Delacroix, an olive-skinned dandy who looked like Byron and was reputed to be the son of Talleyrand. His Sardanapalus had been one of the sensations of the Salon of 1827. We may dismiss him today as a writer's painter, but he had brought a wealth of color and vitality into French painting which is what was needed at the time. With Delacroix came Prosper Mérimée, too sarcastic to be popular but destined to be one of the great story tellers of the nineteenth century. ' Carmen ' and ' Colomba ' are still unborn but he has already mystified the literary world with his ' Théâtre Clara Gazul.' Balzac was there too, affecting an elegance that never came naturally to him, and among others a great burly giant named Dumas, whose weaknesses whatever they may have been did not include an affectation of gentility. This amiable Hercules, who sent all France to the theatre and wrote the greatest epic of friendship in the history of literature, was one of Hugo's most devoted admirers. Years later when that great reputation was on the wane he confessed that he would have sacrificed any one of his sixty-six dramas in exchange for the fourth act of 'Marion Delorme.' The youngest and perhaps the most talented of all the guests was a Monsieur Alfred de Musset, not yet twenty years old but already recognized by Sainte-Beuve as 'un enfant de génie.' Except for David d'Angers, on his way to Weimar to see Goethe, and Lamartine who was at Aix, all the young champions of romance had crowded into the little drawing room of the rue Notre Dame des Champs to acclaim Victor's latest masterpiece.

Among these bearded poets and artists the immaculate figure of Alfred de Vigny is easy to recognize — 'un gentleman d'une tenue parfaite, en habit noir, cravate noire et gilet blanc.' A mute protest perhaps against the outward trappings of romanticism, the velvet tunics and crimson waistcoats that appealed to so many of his contemporaries. He is the least flamboyant of the romantics. The gray blue eyes, the aquiline nose and the unmistakably military bearing suggest an English officer rather than a French poet, and yet there is something in his air of distinction that the society of an officers' mess does not usually lend. His own soirée, which followed so closely upon Victor Hugo's, included the world of fashion as well as the shining lights of art and letters. Alfred de Vigny was at the same time the most exquisite, the most reserved, and the most 'mondain' of the young romantics. No one was more aware of the gentleman in him than Sainte-Beuve, who despite a certain parade of admiration always resented his long-standing friendship with Victor Hugo. Under the subtle influence of Sainte-Beuve the great Victor was gradually being alienated from his aristocratic friend. Vigny himself was perfectly aware of the change. In the spring of 1829, shortly after the reading of ' Marion Delorme' and ' Othello,' he notes in his journal ' the Victor I used to love is no more.' The prophecy of General Hugo, Victor's father, was coming true — ' the child may think like his mother, the man will think like me.' Victor Hugo, brought up to be *plus royaliste que le roi,* was drifting into the camp of the liberals. The refusal of the Government to permit the production of ' Marion Delorme,' on the ground that it was disrespectful to the memory of Louis XIII merely hastened Victor's conversion. In vain did he plead with the King himself for the right to produce his play. Charles X treated him like a wayward child; he offered to increase the pension Hugo was already receiving but he would not permit the play to be acted. It was not Vigny's fault if the Théâtre français decided to substitute his translation of ' Othello ' for the forbidden ' Marion Delorme.' Victor Hugo attended the first night and is said to have applauded vociferously but his comment on the performance in a letter to Sainte-Beuve hardly suggests the warm sympathy of a loyal friend — " Othello has succeeded — not a startling success, but as much as could be expected, and thanks to us."

CHAPTER IV

Cette vieille citadelle de la Rue Richelieu va nous appartenir si nous ouvrons la brèche. VIGNY

Le Théâtre-français s'est rendu, faute d'avoir été secouru à propos et ravitaillé en temps opportun. Dans la soirée du 25 octobre dernier, Attila-Shakespeare en a pris possession avec armes et bagages, enseignes déployées, au fracas de mille fanfares. GUIZOT

VIGNY ALWAYS MAINTAINED THAT IT WAS HIS 'OTHELLO' rather than Victor Hugo's 'Hernani' that struck the first blow for liberty in the theatre and opened the way for a more passionate and a more realistic drama. It was the first time that a literal translation of Shakespeare, as literal that is as a verse translation can be, had been attempted on the French stage. Actually it was neither Vigny nor Victor Hugo but Alexandre Dumas who was the real pioneer in emancipation, but Dumas' 'Henri III et sa Cour' was written in prose, and prose was still regarded as a medium for melodrama rather than tragedy. Writing in 1823 Stendhal complained that there were still three redoubts in the classical position to be carried — the absurd belief in the superiority of poetry over prose, the devotion to the unities, and the ridiculous insistence on dignity rather than appropriateness of language.

One of the strongest allies of the romantics in their battle for liberty was Shakespeare. Up to the time of Vigny's ' Othello' the Shakespeare that France knew was a strange travesty of the real man, even more strange if that be possible than the Shakespeare of Dryden and Nahum Tate. The first mention of him in France is from the pen of Nicholas Clement, royal librarian to Louis XIV. " This English poet," says Nicholas Clement in the catalogue that he compiled for his royal master, " has a pretty lively imagination, he thinks realistically, and he expresses himself with subtlety, but these good qualities are all obscured by the filth which he mixes in his comedies." The first mention of Shakespeare in a French book occurs in the ' Jugements des Savants,' 1685–1686, by Baillet, in which he is mentioned as one of the principal poets of the British islands. It was not, however, until Voltaire's ' Lettres Philosophiques' that any Frenchman had attempted a serious estimate of Shakespeare's genius. Voltaire's first impression of Shakespeare was not materially different from that of his English contemporaries. Shakespeare was a wild untutored genius of tremendous power but utterly without taste (sans la moindre étincelle de bon goût) and without the slightest knowledge of the rules of tragedy. Voltaire goes on to speak of the ' farces monstrueuses' called tragedies, which contain he admits such wonderful scenes that they still hold the stage. Among the monstrosities that he picks out are the suffocating of Desdemona and the unseemly levity of the gravediggers in ' Hamlet.'

Later in life Voltaire's wary enthusiasm for Shakespeare was still further modified. He admired the barbarian but he would have no one praise him except himself, and when his protégé showed some signs of encroaching upon the popularity of Racine and Corneille, Voltaire attacked him with characteristic vehemence. In 1772 the Comte de Catuelan, Letourneur and Fontaine-Malherbe announced a complete translation of Shakespeare. It was to be a magnificent undertaking, dedicated to the young king and including among its list of subscribers the flower of the aristocracy. The first two volumes, which appeared in 1776, inspired Voltaire to write to his friend d'Argental — " Have you by any chance read two volumes by that wretch Letourneur in which he tries to make us believe that Shakespeare is the only model for real tragedy. . . . The worst of it is that the monster has a party in France, and worse still I was myself the first to speak of this Shakespeare; I was the first to show the French a few pearls that I had found in this enormous dung-hill." (July 19, 1776.)

But it was now too late for Voltaire to put out the fire that he had unwittingly kindled. The barbaric Shakespeare in Letourneur's fancy dress was winning his way into all the libraries and drawing-rooms. 'Never had a man of genius penetrated further into the human heart' maintained his translators, and the public seem to have agreed with them. The third volume appeared in 1778 containing the names of 149 new subscribers. By the end of the century Shakespeare the poet had been definitely accepted but

Shakespeare the dramatist was not so easy to acclimatize. Anglomania had long been the fashion in the Parisian salons. Diderot had wept over Clarissa Harlowe, Montesquieu had expatiated on the indomitable English love of freedom. Walpole and Garrick, Sterne and David Hume, had all been received with the greatest cordiality. To be known as a man of the world it was almost necessary to adopt English fashions in dress and deportment. Garrick's recitations from Shakespeare had taken the salons by storm; no one had ever been so moving or so natural. But the theatre-going public was not so easily convinced as the Faubourg St. Germain. It was much more conservative in its taste and much less affected by the prevalent Anglomania.

The adaptation of ' Romeo and Juliet ' which the Chevalier de Chastellux presented at the famous Château de la Chevrette, the rendezvous for men of letters and society, was carefully designed so as not to shock the susceptibilities of the audience. The translator prided himself on having altered much of the intrigue and on having left out all that was comic, and even all that is tragic too, for the Chevalier's play ends merrily as possible. At about the same time ' Othello ' was translated and adapted by one Douin, a captain of infantry. In this version Desdemona dies on the stage but she is stabbed and not smothered. The dagger was the established weapon of French tragedy, and any other method of killing a character on the stage induced an invariable shudder of revolt. Douin was prepared to employ his leisure in giving his compatriots successively the whole of Shakespeare's dramas, "reserving to myself only the liberty of cleansing his plays, both comic and tragic, of pruning them of their superfluities, and of reducing them to the limits of the three unities." Apparently Douin's first venture was not a success for his threat of translating the whole of Shakespeare was never fulfilled.

'Othello' seems to have been a popular play with French audiences. It was presented again in 1776, in 1785, and finally by Ducis, the most devoted of Shakespeare's French admirers, in 1792. Throughout his long life Jean François Ducis set himself the task of popularizing Shakespeare on the French stage. His knowledge of English was very sketchy, but he learnt to love Shakespeare through Letourneur's translation, which he adapted freely to suit his own taste. He presented 'Hamlet' in 1769, 'Romeo and Juliet' in 1772, 'King Lear' in 1783, and 'Othello' in 1792. It was in this version of 'Othello' that Talma achieved one of his greatest successes. "People thought they saw, or rather they did see in M. Talma," says Ducis, "the living Othello, with all the African energy, all the charm of his love, of his truthfulness and of his youth." Dumas complains that Ducis emasculated Shakespeare, and certainly he did take the most extraordinary liberties with the text, but probably he gauged the appetite of his countrymen pretty accurately and gave them as undiluted a Shakespeare as they could stomach. Ducis was a brave man but he was a timid playwright. He was one of the few authors of his generation who would accept no favors from Napoleon, but he did not quite dare to risk the word 'mouchoir' on the French stage, and accordingly he substituted a diamond bandeau for the plebeian handkerchief. Like all his predecessors he balked at the smothering of Desdemona.

Thanks to Ducis Shakespeare had finally won his place in the repertory of the Théâtre français. The last demonstration against him was inspired by the sudden appearance in Paris of an English company. In 1822 a group of actors headed by Penley attempted to produce Shakespeare at the Théâtre Porte St. Martin. Their efforts met with conspicuous failure and the police had to intervene to protect them from the assaults of the mob. The capture of Calais by British troops could not have excited more patriotic fury. The actors were greeted with cries of 'à bas Shakespeare, l'adjutant de Wellington.' The ghost of Voltaire may have chuckled at this outburst but four years later he would have been correspondingly depressed. In 1827 and 1828 another English company including Kemble and Kean, Macready and Harriet Smithson were greeted at the Odéon and later at the Théâtre Favart with the utmost enthusiasm. Dumas announced after seeing them that he felt like a man born blind who had suddenly received his sight. " I realized that in the world of the theatre everything emanated from Shakespeare just as in the real world everything emanates from the sun . . . from that moment my vocation was decided." Victor Hugo and

Vigny, Berlioz and Delacroix, every star in the firma-
ment of romanticism reflected the sunshine of Shakespeare's genius. The language of Shakespeare might
not be understood but there was no mistaking the
torture of Othello or the fury of King Lear. How re-
freshing it was to see kings and queens swayed by the
common passions of humanity. Voltaire had complained that Shakespeare's kings were not sufficiently
kingly; they even talked like ordinary human beings. For that very reason they were wildly applauded
by the irreverent youth of 1830. Delacroix maintained that the most determined classicists had low-
ered their flags before the onslaught of Shakespeare's
genius. The sudden admiration for Elizabethan
drama displayed by Berlioz was a more personal matter. He fell in love with the ravishing Harriet Smithson at first sight, and threatened to commit suicide if
she did not marry him. Eventually she did marry him
and for a while they lived happily in a garret in Montmartre, where they were visited by Alfred de Vigny,
one of their most constant friends. Perhaps he felt
that his experience in international marriage might
be useful to them, but if so he was disappointed. It
were hardly likely that Berlioz, 'a volcano always in
eruption' as Rouget de l'Isle called him, would find
in the charming but utterly untemperamental Harriet Smithson the ideal partner for matrimonial happiness. They separated in 1840, and in 1854 she died.
On the occasion of her death Liszt wrote Berlioz
a letter of condolence containing a curiously appro-
priate epitaph. " You loved her. You put her into

your music. Her task was done." Romantic egoism could go no further.

The English troupe had opened with ' The Rivals ' and ' She Stoops to Conquer ' which were only moderately successful, for Sheridan and Goldsmith did not really appeal to the French mind. It was Shakespeare that the public wanted. " Vite, Messieurs les Anglais," said the critic of the *Débats,* "une des bonnes tragédies de Shakespeare." Messieurs les Anglais promptly obliged with a performance of ' Hamlet ' played by Kemble and Harriet Smithson. The effect was instantaneous. 'A crowd within, a multitude without, and stifling heat in every part of the theatre.' The monumental edition of Letourneur and the innumerable adaptations of Ducis had paved the way for the capture of the Odéon, one of the strongholds of Racine and Corneille, by an English company.

The success of this English company, whose season lasted from September 7, 1827 to July 25, 1828, had caused considerable anxiety in the councils of the Théâtre français. Without Talma, who died in 1826 and who for so many years had been their mainstay, the Théâtre français could hardly hope to attract the public with the pseudo-Greek and Roman tragedies that had satisfied theatregoers under the Empire. The nomination of Baron Taylor, an old regimental friend of Vigny's, to the post of ' commissaire royale près de la Comédie française ' was a fortunate event for the new drama. Baron Taylor was also a friend and admirer of Dumas and Charles Nodier, and he was con-

sequently more than ready to pilot his ship into the
uncharted waters of romanticism. Vigny was known
to be interested in Shakespeare. What could be more
timely, now that the Shakespeare mania was at its
height, than a French ' Othello ' or a French ' Romeo
and Juliet' that really preserved the fire of the original? Vigny's first dramatic venture was a translation of
' Romeo and Juliet,' of which he wrote the last two
acts and his friend Emile Deschamps the first three.
According to Victor Hugo, not perhaps a judicial
critic, it was a most brilliant translation. " Congratulations, my dear Alfred. . . . Your Romeo is admirable, it is the Romeo of Shakespeare, and yet it is yours
too. You needed just as much genius as the great poet
himself to translate him so admirably." The play was
accepted by the Comédie française but it was never
produced, much to Deschamps' disappointment.
Vigny afterwards claimed that Mlle. Mars, who was to
have played the part of Juliet, decided against it on the
ground of her age. " If I were the right age to play
Juliet," she is reported to have said, " I should not
have the talent, but having the talent I am no longer
of the right age." No other actress has stated the
problem more succinctly. Vigny himself was probably
largely responsible for his play never going into rehearsal. Managers found him a difficult author to
please as he had very rigid ideas about the cast, and
on this occasion when he found that another playwright was presenting a version of ' Romeo and Juliet '
at the Odéon doubtless he lost interest in the whole
undertaking. Meanwhile, Deschamps was longing to

see the play produced. Finally he translated the last two acts himself and published his translation, rather to Vigny's annoyance, but it never reached the footlights. Deschamps' nearest approach to dramatic fame was the libretto he wrote for the ' Romeo and Juliet ' of Berlioz.

Vigny undertook the translation of ' Othello ' in a more ardent frame of mind. A copy of the first folio, lent to him by a bibliophile named Robert, whetted his curiosity, and gave him the advantage of working from an authentic text. Taylor proved himself an efficient ally by borrowing 9500 francs for the production from the next year's budget. The painting of the scenery including a gothic chamber, a gothic palace and a gothic street, amounted to 6210 francs. The officials of the Comédie française, if not entirely convinced, were willing to do their best for Shakespeare and Monsieur de Vigny. Mlle. Mars, the most celebrated actress in the company, was pressed into the service of romanticism, and gave a satisfactory performance. She was perhaps, as the critic of the *Quotidienne* remarked, ' a little too ripe ' to be an ideal Desdemona. Vigny would have preferred to give the part to a young actress named Marie Dorval, but unfortunately she was engaged by the Théâtre Porte St. Martin. The actor who played the part of Iago, named Perrier, contributed more than any one else to the success of the play. His conception of Iago — ' une grande âme et un coeur corrompu ' — which was borrowed from the celebrated English actor Young, for whose opinion Vigny had great respect, was exactly suited to the temper of the romantics. Vigny took infinite pains over the rehearsals and he was rewarded by a cordial if not an enthusiastic reception. The play was given thirteen times in 1829 and three times in 1830.

In the introduction that he wrote for the printed text, addressed to a mythical Lord B——, Vigny remarked rather grandiloquently, ' J'ai eu mon soirée, mon cher Lord, et voilà tout.' Actually it had been a ' succès d'estime' rather than a popular success. He had struck a blow for liberty in the theatre by using the fatal word ' mouchoir' and by killing Desdemona on the stage as Shakespeare meant her to be killed, but after all a translation however brilliant can never have the force of an original work. As Dumas put it, "the victory won by Vigny was a victory without result. It was we who were on trial now, not Shakespeare or Goethe or Schiller."

Vigny's introduction contains some interesting reflections of the differences between French and English dramatic poetry. He regrets that whereas in English the drama has three octaves in which to express itself, rhyme, blank verse and prose, in French it has to meet every demand with the alexandrine. When Shakespeare is translated into French, Caliban and the Queen of the fairies, Bottom and Othello, all have to tread the same relentless measure. The alexandrine line serves well enough for the rendering of pure rhetoric, but it is lamentably inadequate for those passages of realism that Shakespeare invariably couches in prose.

ALFRED DE VIGNY

Adieu, beaux bataillons aux panaches flottants!
Adieu, guerre! adieu, toi dont les jeux éclatants
Font de l'ambition une vertu sublime!
Adieu donc, le coursier que la trompette anime,
Et ses hennissements, et le bruit du tambour,
L'étendard qu'on déploie avec des cris d'amour!
Appareil, pompe, éclat, cortège de la gloire!

In this passage Vigny holds his own with Shake-speare: —

Farewell the plumed troop, and the big wars,
That make ambition virtue! O, farewell!
Farewell the neighing steed, and the shrill trump,
The spirit-stirring drum, the ear-piercing fife,
The royal banner, and all quality,
Pride, pomp and circumstance of glorious war!

But when we turn to one of Iago's characteristic speeches the gulf between the English and French is immediately apparent.

La vertu! mot oiseux. C'est de soi qu'on dépend,
Comme un sillon des grains que la main y répand.

This is hardly a satisfactory rendering of Shake-speare's

'Virtue! a fig! 'tis in ourselves that we are thus or thus. Our bodies are our gardens, to the which our wills are gardeners:'

In the last hundred years there have been many French translations of Shakespeare, some of them closer to the original than Vigny's, but within the limits of the alexandrine no one has been more successful.

Vigny's unswerving belief in the dignity of poetry and the moral and intellectual superiority of the poet to every other member of society, finds its first expression in this essay. He compares society to the face of a clock. The hour hand represents the progress of the masses, slow and invisible but none the less sure. The minute hand stands for the enlightened members of society whose progress can just be detected by the naked eye. But there is also a second hand which races around the circle and which represents the winged flight of the poets compared to which the progress of the rest of the world is painfully pedestrian. The superior intelligence of poets and their consequent loneliness is one of Vigny's most cherished theories. He reverts to it again and again. When he was finally elected to the Academy he chose it as the theme of his address, much to the disgust of those of his colleagues who did not have the advantage of being poets themselves.

With the tumultuous success of ' Hernani ' which followed hard upon the heels of ' Othello ' the triumph of romantic drama was complete. The classical-romantic war in the French theatre may be said to have lasted from 1823, when Stendhal published his invidious comparison between Shakespeare and Racine, down to 1830 when Hugo's truculent admirers took possession of the Théâtre français and shouted ' Hernani ' into fame. The significance of the romantic element in literature has been discussed so often that the subject has been worn threadbare. Whether we agree with Goethe that classicism is health and romanticism disease, or whether we accept the dictum of Baudelaire that 'romanticism is the most recent, the most modern and the most vivid expression of the Beautiful,' depends upon our interpretation of this much abused word. Its history, of which Mr. Logan Pearsall Smith has recently made a careful study, shows that it was first introduced into France from England by Letourneur, the translator of Shakespeare, and the Marquis de Girardin, the author of a book on landscape. They found no equivalent for this mot *anglois,* as they called it, in the French language. Romanesque meant 'chimerical' or 'fabulous,' while 'pittoresque' merely suggested a scene that was paintable. The word 'romantic,' says Mr. Logan Pearsall Smith, implies an appeal to the feelings and to the imagination at the same time; it not only describes the scene but the touching impression we receive from it. Both authors enumerate the scenes that in the 18th century were considered romantic, the heaths, the sea, the clouds of the Caledonian landscape, mountains, torrents and waterfalls, and 'le lovely moon' des Anglois. . . . The word soon became fashionable in France, and was included in the Dictionary of the French Academy in 1798, with the definition 'Il se dit ordinairement des lieux, des paysages, qui rappellent a l'imagination les descriptions des poëmes et des romans.'

It was Madame de Stael in her famous book 'De

l'Allemagne' who first pronounced the phrase 'lit-térature romantique' in France. Her long sojourn in Germany and her literary association with such men as A. W. Schlegel was responsible for the German element in French romanticism. Schiller had already been accepted. His celebrated play, 'Die Raüber,' which so terrified Coleridge that he could not go to bed, had been very popular with the French revolutionaries and won for its author the title of French citizen along with Tom Paine and other leading lights of republicanism. Goethe had made his way more slowly. Faust was not at first popular in France and though according to Gautier it 'contained everything and even a little more than everything,' the public did not take to it as they did to 'William Tell,' of which there were six productions in the year 1828 alone. The Germans were not as important as Shakespeare in shaping the destinies of the French romantic drama, but they did open up new vistas of history and they did prove, if any further proof were necessary, that the unities might well be ignored.

In his book on Shakespeare which includes a long review of Vigny's 'Othello,' Guizot complained that the pendulum had swung too far and that the theatre was now in danger of being inundated by weak imitations of Shakespeare and Schiller. 'Macbeth' and 'William Tell' might prove just as disastrous to originality as 'Andromaque' and 'Zaire.' "The beautiful," says Guizot, "can not be imitated. What is imitated are the faults, the external forms, the mannerisms of the great poets." Vigny was not one of the superficial imitators. He was just as anxious as Gautier to throw overboard the unities and to escape the thralldom of Greece and Rome. He was just as much a romantic as Hugo in his longing, unsatisfied but none the less real, to make the world over instead of accepting it and observing it as it was, but he was more of an intellectual than either of them. He did not regard Shakespeare merely as a useful weapon in the struggle for liberty in the theatre. Nor did he draw far-fetched comparisons as Stendhal did between the England of 1590 and the France of 1830. Vigny seized upon Shakespeare because he represented more of life, its beauty and its ugliness, than any author of antiquity. At a time when Gautier and Hugo were thinking only about the emancipation of the theatre from the fetters of convention Vigny was already grappling with the philosophic problem of progress. His journal for 1829 and 1830 is only incidentally concerned with the production of ' Othello.' He is becoming interested in the doctrines of Saint Simon and the ability of the Bourbons to face the rising tide of democracy.

It is true that many of the stock themes of romantic literature crop out in Vigny's writings — the wickedness of civilization, the absurdity of law and custom, the struggle between the individual and society, the right to happiness and the certainty of happiness but for the shackling effect of institutions — but his fine intelligence demanded something more than the bitter expostulation that satisfied so many of his contemporaries. With the exception of Sainte-Beuve he was the most deeply read of any of the romantics.

'Our literature,' he says in the journal 'frequently utters nothing more than the cries of a sick man.' That was the danger to which Goethe was referring when he told Eckerman that romanticism was disease. Carlyle had the same idea in mind when he urged his generation to close their Byrons and to open their Goethes. Salvation lay in doing instead of feeling. The disease of romanticism could be escaped either by plunging head first into the world or, and this was more difficult and less dramatic, by devoting oneself to a career of intense mental activity. Byron was fortunate enough to stumble upon a war of Independence; the Fates were not so kind to Alfred de Vigny. The Revolution of 1830, of which he was an eyewitness offered no clear cut issue. He would have given his life for Charles X or the Dauphin if either of them had come to Paris and played the man, instead of which they idled away the throne at St. Cloud while their soldiers left without orders were being sniped from behind barricades. " They are not coming to Paris where their soldiers are dying for them. Race of Stuarts! I shall stick to my family." So wrote Vigny on July 29th, 1830. On the same day Talleyrand standing on the balcony of his hotel on the corner of the rue St. Florentin and the rue de Rivoli dictated the following note to his secretary. " On the 29th of July, 1830, at precisely five minutes past twelve the elder branch of the Bourbon family ceased reigning over France." Talleyrand's philosophic detachment reflects a cynicism that Vigny's generation never learned to acquire.

CHAPTER V

*En politique je n'ai plus de coeur. Je ne suis pas fâché
qu'on me l'ait ôté, il gênait ma tête.*

VIGNY

No one felt the collapse of the Bourbon monarchy more keenly than Alfred de Vigny. He had not
been one of those who hailed the return of the Bourbons with wild enthusiasm. He had not written patriotic odes like Victor Hugo, nor had he been invited,
as Hugo and Lamartine and Nodier had been, to the
coronation of Charles X at Rheims. If he had been
present at that ostentatiously feudal ceremony he
would probably not have been impressed by the sight
of the elderly prince prostrating himself before the
High Altar. Charles X girt with the sword of Charle-
magne, his brow anointed with oil from the sainte
ampoule, symbolized the ancien régime, and Vigny
was too much a man of his time to believe that any
king could force back the hands of the clock. Furthermore Vigny felt that he had been slighted by the
Bourbons because after twelve years of service in their
behalf he was still only a captain. Consequently when,
at the instigation of Polignac the most shortsighted
minister a king was ever cursed with, Charles X issued
his famous Ordinances dissolving the Chamber and

suspending the liberty of the press, measures which Vigny realized the people would not tolerate, he was not one of those who leapt instinctively to the defence of the monarchy.

His own position was a peculiarly difficult one. The entries in his journal for the 28th and 29th of July, the two critical days, reveal the troubled state of his mind: " Fighting has been going on since this morning. The workmen are as brave as the Vendéens; the soldiers as gallant as the Imperial Guard. What is my duty? To protect my mother and my wife. What am I? A retired captain. I left the service five years ago. The Court has done nothing for me. My writings displease them; they think them seditious. Louis XIII was described in such a way that people often say to me: ' You who are a liberal.' I have received from the Bourbons only one promotion, when I was in the fifth regiment of the guard, and that was a mere matter of seniority. And yet if the King comes back to the Tuileries and if the Dauphin puts himself at the head of his troops I shall go and die with them. The tocsin. I have seen the fire from the attic window. Fire will bring disorder in its wake. Unhappy people, great people. Soldiers — every one of them."

The accession of Louis Philippe, the Duc d'Orléans, seemed to Vigny as it did to so many of his countrymen, a profoundly unsatisfactory sequel to the banishment of Charles X. With all his faults Charles X possessed a certain royal dignity. Even his enemies admitted that he was every inch a king, though unfortunately a stupid king, as he proved by his ill-advised remark that he would rather saw wood than rule like his cousin, the King of England. His successor, Louis Philippe, though not lacking in physical courage, was essentially a bourgeois, and a bourgeois king was too obviously a compromise between the republicans and the monarchists to inspire either devotion or respect. No king ever lent himself more irretrievably to caricature. This 'paysan parvenu,' as Vigny called him, this 'poire couronné,' who sauntered down the rue de Rivoli with a green umbrella tucked under his arm, shaking hands with anybody who happened to recognize him, suddenly found himself King of the French. The monarchy was significantly shorn of its sacred character by the assertion that the new King held his crown from the French people. The Duc d'Orléans in spite of Vigny's contempt was in many ways an admirable compromise candidate. Though he was a royal prince, his father Philippe Egalité had voted for the death of Louis XVI in 1793, while he himself had fought at Jemappes, as he never tired of reminding his courtiers, against the enemies of his country. He was consequently that rare thing, a royal prince with revolutionary sympathies. As far as anybody knew he had made no effort to be king, and he had been discreet enough not to associate too much with the republicans or the monarchists. No one could pretend however that he was a popular choice. A few of the more moderate spirits in Paris including a rising young journalist named Thiers and the veteran banker Laffitte had decided that a constitutional mon-

archy rather than a republic was what France needed
at the moment. The little bespectacled Monsieur
Thiers, as unlikely a kingmaker as the mind of man
could conceive, had galloped off to Neuilly where the
Duke was living to offer him the throne. The Duke
himself was out, but his sister Madame Adelaide let it
be known that he was willing. Thiers hurried back to
Laffitte with the glad tidings; Louis Philippe was
their man.

Thiers' carefully worded announcement 'the King
reigns and does not govern' was calculated to allay
the misgivings of the Liberals. If Lafayette had been
twenty years younger he might have become first
president of France. As it was the old warrior greeted
Louis Philippe at the Hotel de Ville with a kiss of
welcome, a kiss which as Metternich remarked stifled
a republic. The new king gave every evidence of
being anxious to please. He agreed to the title of
King of the French instead of King of France, and
he accepted the tricolor of the Revolution and the
Empire instead of the white banner and the fleur de
lys of the Bourbons. These changes were not fundamental enough to attract or to repel a critical observer like Alfred de Vigny. He noted at once the inherent weakness of the July monarchy, that it was
based neither upon the will of the people nor upon
the right of succession. Vigny decided that he owed
no more devotion to such a government than he owed
to his coachman: 'He drives well or he drives badly,
that is all.'

At the same time though he felt no obligation

towards the new government he was acutely conscious
of his duty as a citizen. Whether the head of the state
were a king or a president, a Bourbon or a Valois,
order had to be preserved. Vigny accordingly joined
the National Guard immediately after the July monarchy was established. It is interesting that while Victor Hugo shut himself up in a garret to finish ' Notre
Dame de Paris,' Vigny the intellectual aristocrat
so often derided for living in an ivory tower should
have been drilling his battalion. While he was never
reconciled to Louis Philippe he could not help being
pleased when the King congratulated him upon the
soldierly bearing of his troops. He even admits after
a review of the National Guard in the Champs de
Mars that for once Louis Philippe looked like a King.
Then he adds in a moment of rare irony, " I thought
him handsome just as Mme. de Sévigné thought
Louis XIV the greatest king in the world after she
had danced with him." Whatever his opinion of
Louis Philippe, Vigny took his duties in the National
Guard very seriously. He dreamed of making his battalion a serious corps independent of intrigue, immune to the flattery of the Court and the factions of
the mob. Nor did he confine himself to dreaming. On
at least one occasion, during a riot, he formed his
battalion into a hollow square, arrested thirty prisoners and brought them into the prefecture of police.

As time went on Vigny became more and more dis-
satisfied with the new régime. The growing power of
industrialism, the cult of prosperity expressed in
Guizot's insistent bleat ' enrichissez vous,' found no

echo in his heart. Apparently the empire of intelligence was no nearer realization under Louis Philippe than it had been under Charles X. The ultra royalists disappeared and their places at Court were taken by bankers and business men. "In a materialist society," observes Vigny, "doctors become gods and financiers kings." Meanwhile the poet was left to fend for himself as he has been under every system of government. To Vigny the complacent indifference of those in power to poets and artists was a serious blot on our civilization. He had already referred to it in his introduction to ' Othello,' and it became the main theme of his next romantic novel.

Perhaps it is hardly accurate to call ' Stello ' a novel. Actually it is a series of romantic biographies in which Vigny traces the fate of three unfortunate poets, Gilbert whom the ancien régime allowed to die of starvation, Chatterton driven to suicide under a constitutional monarchy, and André Chénier the victim of the Reign of Terror. These stories are told in the form of a dialogue between Stello the incarnation of sentiment, and Doctor Noir the epitome of dispassionate reason. Vigny's assumption that the state is responsible for the welfare of its poets, and his insistence upon the altruism of the individual is not particularly convincing. We can hardly believe, as he apparently does, that the individual is rarely at fault and the social order always, and it is certainly not on account of this thesis that anybody today would take the trouble to read ' Stello.' What we admire in the book is the author's talent for telling a story. Much has been writ-

MARIE DORVAL
From a lithograph by Léon Noël

ten about Vigny the poet and Vigny the philosopher
but Vigny the story teller seems to have been neglected. No one is more rapid in his narrative or more
accomplished in setting the scene with a few deft
strokes. Madame de Coulanges and Louis XV in the
Trianon, Gilbert starving in his attic, the ghastly
suppers in the prison of St. Lazare with the tumbrils
rolling by outside, these scenes are etched into our
memory with flawless precision. Has any other novelist or any historian recreated the horrors of the Reign
of Terror so poignantly as Alfred de Vigny? His
economy of phrase is one of his great virtues. He is
not one of those authors who tell the reader everything, who even buttonhole him in the middle of
the story to analyze the sensations he should be ex-
periencing. He is the master of the ' conte.' His style
is never obtrusive; it has the sinuous grace of the
athlete whose muscles ripple smoothly below the surface rather than the ponderous biceps of the professional strong man.

' Stello ' appeared first in three instalments in a new
periodical called the *Revue des Deux Mondes*.
Vigny was among the earliest contributors. The review had been founded early in 1831 by François
Buloz, a very insistent and a very successful editor who
never admitted discouragement or idleness in himself or his contributors. From the date of its birth,
February 15, 1831, when it flashed upon the world
in a beautiful salmon dress decorated with a vignette
by Tony Johannot representing America stark naked
offering Europe an olive branch, the *Revue des*

Deux Mondes has played a considerable part in French literature. Vigny, George Sand, Balzac and Sainte-Beuve and a host of others, regarded it almost as their own child. Buloz wrote practically nothing himself but he had more effect upon public opinion than all the academies in France. Though he was a hard taskmaster — his contributors called him ' l'ours de la revue ' — he and Vigny were always on excellent terms. Buloz was occasionally bothered by Vigny's anxiety to get the work of his friends noticed in the review, for no one was more generous in lending à hand to other authors, but Vigny was too useful a contributor to be antagonized and he usually had his way. Sainte-Beuve insinuates that he and Buloz used to laugh over Vigny's literary sterility but during the years 1830 to 1835 Vigny was positively prolific. ' Stello,' ' Servitude et Grandeur,' and three plays, ' La Maréchale d'Ancre,' ' Quitte pour la Peur,' and ' Chatterton,' all fall within these five years. They were the most crowded years of his life. During this period he flirted with the doctrines of Saint-Simon, and for a short time at any rate he was intimate with Buchez, one of the most ardent of Saint-Simon's followers. He even wrote verses glorifying the dignity of labor and acclaiming the great social harmony of the future, which are entirely and perhaps fortunately unlike the rest of his poetry.

> *La vie est un vaste atelier*
> *Ou, chacun faisant son métier,*
> *Tout le monde est utile.*

ALFRED DE VIGNY

On agit d'un commun effort,
Et du faible aidé par le fort
* La tâche est plus facile.*
Dieu du travail, Dieu de la paix
C'est à l'oeuvre que tu parais:
* Le feu, ta main l'allume.*
L'Ouvrier voit, dès son berceau,
Ta grande main sur le manteau,
* Ton genou sous l'enclume!*

Buchez advocated a system of universal fraternity
to be achieved through membership in voluntary as-
sociations, which he believed to be synonymous with
universal happiness. It is difficult to think of Vigny
being carried away by such visionary schemes but for
a year or two he certainly was influenced by the economic idealism of Saint-Simon's disciples. His conception of the king as a glorified coachman is directly borrowed from Buchez. Vigny also shared the popular
enthusiasm over Lamennais. He wrote for his paper
l'Avenir, and he begged Montalembert to arrange an
interview with him.

At the same time that he was working for Buloz
and lending a sympathetic ear to the various prophets
of the moment, he was writing plays for Marie Dorval
with whom he had fallen desperately in love. For the
moment we will confine ourselves to his literary ventures, always remembering that biography is necessarily false in that it gives the impression that a man
does only one thing at a time. Vigny was not what is
popularly known as a man of action but his mind was

so active, his emotions so alert, that his life was more variegated than it seemed to his contemporaries.

One of the things that made most impression upon Vigny during the three days of street fighting that marked the end of the Bourbon monarchy was the behavior of the regular army. He notes in the journal several examples of characteristic loyalty and in particular the action of a certain Captain Le Motheux who had resigned his commission on the day that Charles X issued his detested ordinances. On the following day fighting in the streets broke out and he at once requested that his letter be ignored. That evening his company was cut off from the rest of his battalion; he refused to surrender and was shot. Vigny seized upon this episode for the final story of ' Servitude et Grandeur Militaires.'

' La Canne de Jonc ' is the story of the life and death of Captain Renaud, the most interesting and the most convincing of all Vigny's characters. Captain Renaud is the stoic who has learned wisdom from experience. As a child he had had the most intense admiration for Napoleon but this admiration had been shattered by his happening to overhear a conversation between the Emperor and Pope Pius VII. The pope had been brought to Fontainebleau and was being kept there virtually as a prisoner until he should yield to the imperial demands. Napoleon had tried to bully the Holy Father into submission, but his bluster had been punctured by the two words — ' commediánte,' ' tragediánte.' Suddenly the feet of clay of this idol that had so long dominated Europe were glaringly revealed. The man was nothing more than an actor, and upon the pope his acting had failed to make any impression. In the place of Napoleon the young soldier learns to worship a new hero, Admiral Collingwood, whose prisoner he is for four long years. Vigny's Collingwood is a French conception of all that is best in the English character. He is dominated by a devastating sense of duty but beneath his Anglo-Saxon reserve lurks a real tenderness and a delicate consideration for others. Actually Collingwood was not the incarnation of selflessness that Vigny believed him to be but he serves very well as a contrast to Napoleon. While Renaud is railing at the fate which has delivered him into the hands of the English he learns from Collingwood's own lips that he too is a prisoner, that he has been at sea for forty years, during which time he has not spent ten consecutive days at home. His children are growing up without knowing him. Again and again he begs to be relieved of his command but every request is met by the same reply: 'You will continue to remain at sea.' A spirit of abnegation, of uncomplaining patriotism like that of Collingwood, pervaded the remainder of Renaud's life. At one moment he is tempted by fellow prisoners in Gibraltar to escape, but his sense of honor, for he is on parole, comes to his rescue, and he swims back to his floating prison. " When I found myself on board again I clung to the mast as a sanctuary which saved me from dishonor, and at the same moment realizing the magnitude of my sacrifice I fell on my knees, I pressed my forehead against the mast and burst into tears." Immediately afterwards he is exchanged but instead of thrusting himself upon Napoleon's attention he welcomes the obscurity of the ranks. Collingwood's advice had borne fruit: " Devote yourself to an ideal rather than to a man. Love for one's country is a big enough ideal to fill your heart and to possess your mind."

So he found, but there was one bitter experience in the campaign of 1814 which supplemented Collingwood's noble stoicism. In a night attack upon a Russian outpost he had the misfortune to kill a child of fourteen — one of those boys who occasionally held commissions in the Russian army. As a result of this experience he conceived a loathing of bloodshed, and afterwards instead of a sabre he carried a bamboo cane which had dropped from the dying hand of the boy he had killed. Henceforth he was always known by his soldiers as old ' canne de jonc.' Unambitious, unostentatious and therefore unnoticed, he did his duty without reward or distinction, but there was no officer more beloved by his men or more genuinely devoted to their welfare. In the street fighting of July 29 he withdrew his company in good order from the Place de la Bastille to the Champs de Mars, where he received his death wound from a small boy who had been bribed by two workmen to fire a pistol at him point blank. As soon as he realized what he had done the child was stricken with remorse. He tended his victim up to the last moment. The good captain bore him no malice, but on the contrary he bequeathed to him a certain sum of money for his education and maintenance on the condition that he should not become a soldier.

In the character of Captain Renaud, tempered by adversity, Vigny is perhaps idealizing himself. The patient unrequited devotion to his profession is certainly autobiographic. He always hugged the delusion that the Monarchy had been ungrateful to him just as the Empire had been to Captain Renaud. The reflections on Honor scattered throughout the narrative are most characteristic. " L'Honneur, c'est la pudeur virile," " Il y a quelque chose d'aussi beau qu'un grand homme, c'est un homme d'honneur," etc. Isolate these passages and they may sound stilted — the world has an instinctive distrust of protestations of honor — but woven as they are into the fabric of Vigny's philosophy they can not be laughed aside as the extravagance of a disgruntled aristocrat. Vigny sincerely believed that in the universal shipwreck of creeds and faiths there was nothing left to cling to but ' l'amour du bien-être ' or ' l'honneur.' By Honor he means conscience, an exalted conscience, a respect for oneself and for the beauty of one's life carried almost to the plane of passion. There is nothing new in this faith. It is innate in all of us independent of time, place and religion. The only difficulty about it in Vigny's mind is that it is found in its purest form in the army, and the army as he thought was fast becoming an anachronism. At any rate, it was too far removed from the main stream of national activity to be really effective as a model for the good life.

Another reflection of contemporary events is found in his play ' La Maréchale d'Ancre' which he wrote between the first of August and the end of September 1830, when the hue and cry against the ministers of Charles X was at its height. The scene is laid in 1614 in the reign of Louis XIII. Concini, the Italian favorite who was made Maréchal d'Ancre, and his wife Léonora, share the favor of the king and the hatred of the people. The reference to Polignac, the favorite of Charles X, is very thinly disguised.

The theme of the play, the abolition of the death penalty, is hardly dramatic but Vigny introduced a variety of other elements more calculated to insure a box office success. The part of Léonora Galigai, la Maréchale d'Ancre, was written for Marie Dorval whom he already considered the leading tragic actress of the day. To give her talents full scope he had coated his political thesis with a rich flavor of romanticism. A passionate love story, a duel in the dark in which neither adversary is able to see whether the other has been wounded, distracted the attention of those for whom the stupidity of the Court on the eve of a revolution was too painfully obvious to be dramatic. Vigny wrote a short introduction for his play in which, rather like Bernard Shaw, he enumerated the ideas that he intended to expound. Among these ideas we may notice his theory of destiny. Destiny is something " against which we are always struggling, but which invariably vanquishes us as soon as Character weakens and which relentlessly leads us to mysterious ends, often to expiation, by ways that are impossible to predict." Destiny and Honor were the two themes which came to engross more and more of his attention. They were the two pillars upon which he reared his system of stoical philosophy.

The play was produced on June 21, and again on June 25, 1831. Actually there were two first nights as Mlle. George to whom the part of Léonora Galigai had been assigned had laced herself so tightly the first evening that she was unable to finish the performance. Vigny was again disappointed, not that Mlle. George was a failure but he had written the part for Marie Dorval and no one else would have suited him. Mlle. George indeed was a very talented actress, and still in the heyday of her beauty. She had the further distinction of having been at various times the mistress of Napoleon, Lucien and Jerome Bonaparte — she seems to have had a weakness for the family — also of Talleyrand, Murat and Dumas.

Marie Dorval on the contrary was a young actress who had made a certain name for herself in melodrama, but who was quite unknown in the fashionable world. The audiences of the Théâtre Porte St. Martin knew her as a hard working actress with a raucous voice who was occasionally very effective in emotional roles. No one except Vigny would have dreamed of comparing her with the great actresses of the Comédie française, but already in 1830 she was

to him 'la première tragédienne existante . . . pas-
sionnée et spirituelle.' Though he was the first to dis-
cern her great histrionic talent it took him seven years
to learn that she was not the Egeria his imagination
had so fondly and so deliberately conceived.

CHAPTER VI

Et, plus ou moins, la Femme est toujours Dalila.

VIGNY

MARIE DORVAL, DAUGHTER OF MARIE BOURDAIS AND Joseph Charles Delaunay, was born in 1798 at Lorient, in Brittany. Her father and mother, who belonged to a troupe of strolling players, had forgotten to get married until she was born when the error was finally rectified. Her stage career began at the age of four and it lasted until her death in 1849. As a child she toured the country from Lorient to Strasbourg leading that life of privation and drudgery, punctuated by flashes of success, that has always been the lot of strolling players. Her mother was one of those dreadful parents who insist upon dramatizing the most trifling fault of their children as a deadly sin. " Vous me faites mourir de chagrin," she would say rolling her eyes to heaven, and Marie much too sensitive as it was would take her mother's histrionic outburst literally and spend the night in a paroxysm of tears, praying God to give her back the mother she had assassinated. A more disastrous method of dealing with a sensitive child can hardly be imagined. Thanks to her mother Marie became a permanent slave to her emotions. She was passionate in her affections, passionate in her art, and passionate in her religious exaltation. As she never knew how to control herself, and never wanted to if she had known, her life developed an intensity beyond all human endurance.

By the time she was fourteen she had already tasted success in the part of Fanchette in ' Le Mariage de Figaro.' To her great sorrow she owned only one stage costume, a little white dress upon which, whenever she played Fanchette, she would sew an edging of red calico to give the proper Spanish touch. If two plays were being given on the same evening, as very often happened, Marie would hurriedly unpick the red calico during the intermission so as to appear in the next piece in what seemed a new dress. She was married at sixteen to a man twenty years older than herself, an actor of no talent named Allan Dorval, with whom she toured the provinces in comic opera without success. Her hoarse voice which was so strangely moving in melodrama was completely unsuited to the vivacious comic parts she was compelled to play. In 1811 the company played for the first time in Paris, and there she saw the great Talma in Hamlet. By going without supper for two or three days she scraped up enough money to buy a seat in the gallery. Never had she felt the imperious call of her profession more profoundly. If only she could be delivered from the hated thraldom of comedy she felt she might move audiences as Talma had moved her by his performance of Hamlet. The chance came sooner than she expected. One evening at Strasbourg the actress who had been engaged to play Beaumar-

chais' ' La Mère Coupable ' broke her leg. The manager asked Marie Dorval to take the part, and she
played it with conspicuous success. From then on she
dreamed of nothing but Paris. Eventually with three
small children she found her way to a miserable lodg-
ing in the Latin Quarter. Her husband in the meantime had drifted to St. Petersburg with another troupe
where he died in 1819, leaving her nothing to live on
but an unrecognized talent. With infinite difficulty
she secured a hearing with Lafont, the actor-manager
of the Comédie française, who had her recite for
him one or two scenes from ' Andromaque.' ·Suddenly
he interrupted her: " My dear child, you were not
intended for tragedy. Go and learn the part of Dorine
in ' Tartuffe,' and come back to me." With the last
twenty centimes she bought a copy of ' Tartuffe,'
learned the part and recited it to Lafont's satisfaction.
His reward was more cruel than his previous indifference. He sent her for further training to the Con-
servatory, the place of all others where her emotion-
alism would be cribbed, cabined and confined.

Luckily she had a friend in Paris, Potier the well-
known comedian, who remembered her as a child at
Lorient and who now rescued her from the Conserva-
tory and opened a way for her at the Porte St. Martin,
the home of melodrama. Even then it was some time
before the stilted dramas of the day allowed her talents to reveal themselves. The critics were very
cautious. They were tempted to call her a great actress but her technique was so unconventional that
they hardly dared praise her whole-heartedly. Dor-

val's forte was her naturalness, and she was always being compelled to speak the most unnatural dialogue. Her instinct for reality was infallible. Such phrases as 'que vois-je' and 'où m'égarai-je' always stuck in her throat, though they came perfectly naturally to the lips of the celebrated actors of the Comédie française. On one occasion when she was to act the part of a woman who asphyxiates herself, she bought a brazier and some coal and sitting near the window so as to be able to get relief at the last moment she proceeded to inhale the fumes. But for the intervention of some attentive friends the experiment might well have proved fatal. This incident gives us the clue to her immense popularity; she was the founder in France of a new school of realistic acting. Rachel was to prove an even more conspicuous example of this new realism, but unlike Rachel, Marie Dorval was condemned to waste her talent on extravagant melodramas, in which she had to lend verisimilitude to scenes that were inherently false.

A good example of these fantastic melodramas was 'Trente Ans ou la Vie d'un Joueur,' a play which was enormously popular a hundred years ago and which is still occasionally given as a museum piece. It is an adaptation of one of the fantastic tales of Hoffman who was almost as much of a god to the romantics as Sir Walter Scott. In this play acting with Frédérick Lemaître, the matinée idol of his generation, Marie Dorval broke down all opposition. Lemaître and Dorval were recognized as the most convincing, the most harrowing lovers on the stage. Other triumphs followed in quick succession — ' La Fiancée de Lammermoor,' ' Marino Faliero ' by Casimir Delavigne, and ' Faust,' adapted by Charles Nodier and an inconspicuous gentleman named Merle. Monsieur Merle's only claim upon posterity is that he became Marie Dorval's husband. Why she should have married him no one ever knew. He was an indifferent playwright with expensive tastes which he was unable to gratify, but he was the ideal *mari complaisant* who goes away on long journeys and never interferes with his wife's affairs. Some credit is due to him for the real ingenuity he displayed in never discovering his wife in compromising situations.

Vigny's first acquaintance with Marie Dorval dates from about 1829. He had written ' La Maréchale d'Ancre ' with her in mind but the influence of Mlle. George, who also wanted the part, was too strong for him to overcome. As Vigny gracefully expressed it, Marie Dorval was queen of the theatre only by reason of her talent, and talent without intrigue was unfortunately not omnipotent. In the spring of 1831 she was acting in ' l'Incendiaire,' a rabid anti-clerical play in which a royalist bishop persuades a young girl to set fire to the factory of a republican industrialist. Vigny had no illusions about the merit of the play. Aside from the blasphemy, which scandalized Jews and Protestants as well as Catholics, it was utterly insignificant. There could be no greater proof of Marie Dorval's art than her ability to make such nonsense supremely moving. In the confession scene she reduced everybody to tears, not only the men, women and children, but even the journalists and the claque. Alfred de Vigny did not miss one performance. Night after night he would steal away from the quiet little apartment in the rue d'Artois to enjoy a debauch of sentiment at the Porte St. Martin. What a contrast there was between the good, placid, dull, Lydia enjoying ill health on the sofa at home, and Marie Dorval devastated with emotion greeting a host of admirers in her dressing room. One evening she happened to say to him that she was mystified by a woman in black who had been present at several performances and who without lifting her veil never ceased wiping her eyes. The next day Vigny appeared with the mysterious stranger, still heavily veiled, who in a voice choking with emotion congratulated the actress on her magnificent performance. Marie begged to know the name of her admirer. The lady lifted her veil; it was La Malibran, the greatest opera singer of her day, whose picture Dorval had carried with her ever since she was a child.

By a happy chance Vigny had enabled two of the greatest artists of the day to discover one another. It was the kind of delicate attention in which he excelled. For the first few years of their acquaintance Vigny's relations with Marie Dorval were scrupulously correct. The first effect of love, says Pascal, is to inspire reverence. No one had ever treated Marie Dorval with such charming courtesy. She who had been married when she was a child, who had had lovers before she knew what the word meant, was suddenly surrounded with an atmosphere of respectful adoration. Vigny would read his poems and confide his inmost thoughts to her but still he treated her as a *princesse lointaine*. He never paraded her in public, or sent her bouquets to the theatre, or even took her out to dinner. A complimentary article in the *Revue des Deux Mondes* was the limit of his demonstrativeness. If it was all a new experience for Marie Dorval it was at least equally exciting for Alfred de Vigny. Sainte-Beuve sneered at him for living in a perpetual seraphic hallucination. Neither the brilliant Delphine Gay nor the stolid Lydia approximated his ideal, but when he saw Marie Dorval on the stage in one of her scenes of passionate tenderness she seemed to him the very incarnation of his dream.

Such people as Sainte-Beuve might wonder how the fastidious gentleman could fall in love with an actress of the boulevards who was not even beautiful — she described herself as ' pas belle mais pire ' — and who had a voice that even her admirers admitted was sometimes harsh and unmusical. The explanation is not difficult. Neither had been in love before meeting the other. Alfred de Vigny had indulged in a chaste passion for some ethereal creatures of his imagination, and Marie Dorval had had passing affairs with the heroes of melodrama. Their marriages had not exactly been failures but they had not been the culmination of romantic love. Vigny had married a woman who never troubled to explore the deeper recesses of his nature, and Dorval had married first an insignificant actor and then an insignificant gentleman of leisure neither of whom was capable of understanding a woman of her temperament. The critics might insist upon her vulgarity and her provincial accent but she had a way of throwing herself into life that was peculiarly fascinating to a man of Alfred de Vigny's habitual reserve. Outwardly they appeared to be poles asunder but below the surface they had much in common. They were both highly sensitive; one happened to surrender to the senses while the other trod them under foot. All that was pinched and starved in Vigny's own nature was suddenly revealed to him in Marie Dorval in a riot of glorious abundance. In the journal Vigny describes his life in three words — *aimer, inventer, admirer.* The day when enthusiasm, love adoration and devotion had ceased to exist he would dig down into the middle of the earth, fill the hole with five hundred thousand barrels of powder, and blow the world into a myriad pieces. The same three words — *aimer, inventer, admirer,* apply equally well to Marie Dorval's career. Without love her expansive nature would have withered. She needed to create the emotion on the stage, and she needed also the warm sunshine of applause and admiration. To love and to be loved, to be keenly and perpetually aware of beauty, was essential to Marie Dorval as it was to Alfred de Vigny. Dimly she realized that his devotion was more complimentary than the brusque methods of her other admirers. When Dumas, 'le bon chien Dumas' as she called him, became too ardent in his affections she told him he must learn to make love like Monsieur de Vigny.

On one occasion just after the July revolution, in which Dumas claimed to have risked his life on the barricades, he burst in upon her with the manuscript of ' Antony,' a play in which she afterwards made a tremendous success. Her greeting seemed to him unnecessarily formal.

" Why can't you kiss me? " he asked.

" I am like Marion Delorme: I have taken up virginity again."

" Impossible! "

" On my word of honor. I am becoming ' sage.' "

" And who on earth has made you do that? "

" Alfred de Vigny."

" You love him? "

" Yes, more than I can tell you."

" And what does he do to keep you in love with him? "

" He writes poetry for me."

" In that case, my dear, let me congratulate you. First of all Vigny is a poet of immense talent, secondly he is a real gentleman, while I am only a mulatto. . . ."

Incidentally Dumas was intensely proud of his negro blood. He was quite incapable of entering into the rarefied new world into which Vigny was inducting Marie Dorval but he was an astute enough observer to note that the popular actress was really in love. " There are certain men," she told him, " one does not deceive, they are the men of genius; and if you do deceive them you pay for it." Dumas was appropriately impressed.

"But of course," she added, "it may not last forever. If I should change my mind some day I shall write to you."

"To me?"

"Yes, to you."

"Before anyone else?"

"To you first of all, you know how fond of you I am, 'mon bon chien.'" And with this admirable understanding between them Dumas proceeded to read his new play. The last act did not suit her so he spent the night in Monsieur Merle's study rewriting it. The next morning as soon as she woke up she called him to come into her bedroom and read what he had written. It was satisfactory.

Such was the charming impulsive creature before whom Alfred de Vigny prostrated himself. To him she was a great actress, 'triste, simple, et terrible,' a Shakespearian heroine, one of those victims of society like Cordelia and Desdemona who are forever being broken on the relentless wheel of destiny. Dumas' genially cynical estimate may have been closer to reality, but for a year or two at least Vigny succeeded in breathing life into the ethereal being his imagination had substituted for the frailty of flesh and blood. If only Marie Dorval had been content with the distant homage that Vigny so gladly yielded her! If only she had not suddenly swept away the cloud capped towers and gorgeous palaces he had been at such pains to erect! One abrupt question and the dream vanished — "quand les parents de monsieur le comte viendront-ils demander ma main?"

ALFRED DE VIGNY

Even an Alfred de Vigny could not persist in Platonic affection under that provocation.

The year 1833 was to prove an eventful one in the lives of the Romantics. The young poets who up till then had edified their contemporaries by their exemplary conduct suddenly decided that love was more sacred than marital fidelity. It was in the Carnival of 1833 that Victor Hugo, hitherto the most correct of young husbands, fell in love with Juliette Drouet. In the same year Sainte-Beuve became infatuated with Madame Victor Hugo, Musset and George Sand embarked upon the most completely documented liaison in history, and Vigny surrendered to the greatest passion of them all. He was not one of those men who thrive on intrigue. The constant strategy necessitated by an illicit relationship revolted him. He was too lacking in resiliency, too much a gentleman in the best sense of the word, to throw himself with any gusto into the Bohemian life of his mistress. It may be possible for some men without loss of self-respect to divide their lives into separate compartments but Vigny was not one of them. No one was more incapable of playing a part. The easy familiarity of the stage either delights the layman or it disgusts him. Vigny was disgusted. It made him uncomfortable to shake hands with Monsieur Merle, who was himself indifferent to Vigny's relations with his wife, and it made him still more uncomfortable to see Marie Dorval surrounded by the riff-raff that a popular actress inevitably attracts. To see the woman whom he had placed on a pedestal *tutoyer* anybody and everybody was more of a shock than the twentieth century can easily imagine. Vigny had the gentleman's dislike for a noisy ill-mannered society of which Marie Dorval's court of admirers was largely composed. He had a way of confining his conversation to the one phrase " c'est charmant," which seemed to them peculiarly ridiculous. As a lover he was strangely diffident, and Marie Dorval was not accustomed to diffident lovers. She who aroused outbursts of passion from other men was bewildered by Vigny's delicate caresses. At first she was amused, then flattered, and finally bored. From the beginning of their liaison Vigny realized that he was storing up nothing but unhappiness for himself. Early in the year 1833 we come upon this entry in the journal: " When we find ourselves attracted by a woman, before going any further we ought to ask ourselves: who are her friends, what is her way of life? On the answer to these questions depends all one's future happiness." Such counsels of sagacity are easier to inscribe in a journal than to practise in life. The poet may say to himself ' a sea rolls between us, our different past,' but when the burning moment comes the different past is easily dimmed by the almost intolerable ecstasy of a common present.

Vigny was so absorbed in his mistress that he hardly noticed that she was far more absorbed in her career. Lovers were merely incidental adventures in her life. Perhaps she wrote to Dumas as she had promised, but whether Vigny's immediate successor was Dumas or Jules Sandeau, or some unknown actor is

of no consequence. She was incapable of being faithful to any one man. Tumultuous scenes of recrimi-
nation and repentance followed each other with sick-
ening regularity. After one of these scenes Vigny
writes to her: "I entrust you to the protection of
your love, your honour, and your goodness." Troilus
could not have written Cressida a letter of more
pathetically misplaced confidence. It was not that
Marie Dorval took a wilful pleasure in tormenting
him; it was merely that she had never learned how
to maintain any emotional equilibrium. Life had
taught her a great deal but it had not taught her the
meaning of the word constancy. Fontaney, a minor
poet of the period who afterwards eloped with one
of Dorval's daughters, maintains that Vigny tyran-
nized over her, but Fontaney was a poor creature and
his comments on Vigny are invariably unfriendly.
Marie Dorval described Fontaney as a man of a little
talent, very little courage and no health. Probably
there were moments when she grew weary of Vigny's
elaborate politeness and of his incessant emphasis
upon honor. He persisted in thinking that 'l'honneur' was the rudder by which everyone steered their
course through life. Long after other religions had
crumbled away he believed that the creed of honor
would still be standing four square before the world.
Certainly it was the guiding star in his own life, but
as far as Marie Dorval was concerned he might as
well have preached to her the divine right of kings.
Passion of every kind, good as well as evil, she understood, but renunciation and self-control were virtues

that never swam into her ken. Vigny struggled val-
iantly to adjust himself to the idea of her infidelity.
In his journal for 1833 he writes — "Love that is
physical and only physical pardons all infidelity . . .
but you, spiritual love, passionate love, you can forgive nothing." It was no easy task for a man of his
temper to pretend that even physical love was not
disturbed by the intrusion of unfaithfulness.

In the midst of his disillusionment Vigny wrote
his only comedy, 'Quitte pour la Peur,' in which he
states the case gracefully but effectively for the erring
wife. It was a protest against a husband's authority
over his wife under all conditions, even when the
husband was notoriously unworthy of it. Vigny was
the first man of his generation who as much as
brushed the hem of the feminist movement. George
Sand was the only author of distinction who had
previously broached such problems. Vigny referred
to his comedy as a bagatelle, but a bagatelle with an
undercurrent of seriousness. The play was written
for Dorval who acted it in a benefit, but it was not a
success. Either it was too intimate for the great stage
of the opera where it was produced, or else the public
was not yet ripe for a problem play even when it was
disguised as an eighteenth century comedy.

Shortly after the production of 'Quitte pour la
Peur' Marie Dorval started on a long tour of the
provinces. Vigny was desperately unhappy. He begged
her to write to him regularly, and she answered that
her daughter would communicate with him from
time to time. "What! You think it will be enough to

have Louise write to me from time to time. If you want to torture me that is the way to do it. . . . No, no, no, I need your handwriting, the trace of your hand on the paper, every single day of my life, your handwriting and only yours and let no one else come between us. How cruel of you to accuse me, me of all people, of not helping you enough in your career! You know my life, what more could I do. But you will soon see, if you will only trust me, how much I can still do for you." While he was being tortured by the indifference of his mistress, his mother whom he adored as only a Frenchman can was struck down by apoplexy. She managed to drag out her life for another three years but they were years of terrible anxiety for him. Her suffering and her fits of temper, usually directed at Lydia the docile daughter-in-law, made his home life almost unbearable. The pages of the journal reveal to us how much Vigny and his mother had in common. They were alike in their pride, in their loneliness, and in the inarticulateness of their affections. For Vigny and probably for his mother too there was no comparison between the adequacy of the written word and the stumbling incoherence of speech.

Between his mother and his wife, both invalids and both utterly dependent upon him, for Lydia's father the eccentric millionaire was completely detached from them, Vigny had a hard struggle to provide for his family. Whatever he made out of his books and his plays went into the family exchequer. No wonder that he could not offer Marie Dorval expensive dinners. And yet he managed to extract a certain satisfaction or at least a comforting self-respect out of his enforced economies. He actually thanked God that the Revolution had robbed his father and grandfather of their wealth since the loss of the family fortune had enabled him to experience the pleasure of supporting his mother by his own efforts, and the fact that she was entirely ignorant of his sacrifices made the pleasure still more exquisite.

While Vigny was watching over the sick bed of his mother and of his wife, his mistress was constantly reproaching him for his failure to get her into the Comédie française. In the summer of 1832 he fell a victim to the plague of cholera which swept over Paris during that year. During his illness he burned several unfinished plays for fear that some overzealous editor might publish them with all their imperfections after his death. In 1833 he did manage to produce ' Quitte pour la Peur,' but sophisticated drawing room comedy was not the kind of play in which Marie Dorval's talents showed to best advantage. Immediately afterwards she started on a long tour of the provinces during which Vigny wrote her ardent letters begging for crumbs of affection, and at the same time warning her in a rather magisterial way against her two enemies — ' la gaieté bruyante et la colère.' Violent gusts of temper and gaiety were equally incomprehensible to him. If he made the mistake of assuming that intimacy justified the pose of a schoolmaster no one paid for his mistake more dearly.

In the meantime he was doing his utmost to induce his friend Taylor, now manager of the Comédie française, and Buloz, who had taken Taylor's place as commissaire royal, to open the doors of their theatre for Marie Dorval. The prejudice against an actress of the boulevards was not easy to overcome. Popular success at the Porte St. Martin was by no means an open sesame to the Théâtre français. Vigny had wanted Marie Dorval for his ' Othello ' and ' La Maréchale d'Ancre,' but Mlle. Mars and Mlle. George had been too strongly entrenched to be dislodged. Early in 1834 he was able to write to her in Rouen, where she was then playing, that he had finally secured the coveted engagement for her. " Promise that you are going to be nice when you come back," says the anxious lover, but the fact that he had his doubts is significant. He must have known that gratitude was a negligible factor in their relationship.

Dorval's first appearance at the Comédie française happened to be in a trivial play which failed to justify her tremendous reputation on the boulevards, but on the twelfth of February, 1835, she finally came into her own in the rôle of Kitty Bell, the romantic heroine of Vigny's ' Chatterton.' No actress ever earned her success more courageously. ' Chatterton ' was obviously too far removed from Racine and Corneille to please the conservatives, and it may well have seemed too lacking in vivid incident to suit the young enthusiasts who had hailed the romantic dramas of Hugo and Dumas. At the first reading before the

actors of the Comédie française the play was unani-
mously condemned. Actors are notoriously bad judges
of plays. On this occasion they probably felt, and not
altogether unjustly, that the public which had rev-
elled in the glorious panache of 'La Tour de Nesle'
and 'Hernani' would be completely bewildered by
Vigny's low-keyed tragedy, in which the only sem-
blance of action was the hero's suicide at the end of
the last act. It was only through the intervention of
the Duc d'Orléans, who always interested himself
in the affairs of the Comédie française, that the play
ever went into rehearsal. The actors fought the production step by step. They even grumbled, quite
inconsistently considering that they believed the play
doomed to failure, when they found that the principal part was to be given to Marie Dorval a newcomer
instead of Mlle. Mars the acknowledged favorite.

The problem of selecting the cast for any play given
at the Comédie française seems to have been a matter
of almost national importance. Cabinet ministers and
royalty itself took the keenest interest in the production. The Minister of Fine Arts, whom Vigny happened to meet at the Opera, congratulated him upon
securing the services of Mlle. Mars for his new play.

"But it is not Mlle. Mars who is creating the role
of Kitty Bell," explained Vigny, "but Madame
Dorval."

A few days later at a ball at the Tuileries which
Vigny attended, the King broached the same subject.
"Allow me to congratulate you, Monsieur de Vigny,
upon the great success that awaits you, and upon

the happy choice you have made in Mlle. Mars for the principal part. She is an excellent actress, and the Queen and I shall look forward to applauding her in her new role." Once again Vigny explained with admirable patience that though Mlle. Mars was an excellent actress he had decided upon Marie Dorval for the rôle of Kitty Bell. The King could only wish him success but he warned him a little coldly that he might run into certain difficulties. The royal prophecy proved to be perfectly correct. The conspiracy against Vigny and Marie Dorval was only broken by the overwhelming success of the first night.

In casting about for a suitable play for Marie Dorval, Vigny had decided to dramatize the last days of Chatterton's life. He had already told the story, or rather a romanticized version of the story, in 'Stello.' In less than three weeks, seventeen nights to be exact, he composed the play that was to prove to a sceptical public that Marie Dorval was the greatest actress of the age. 'Chatterton' has been called 'the declaration of the rights of the poet,' but it is actually more than that. It is a diatribe against the Philistine who invariably destroys what he cannot understand. The poet, already in the last stages of poverty, has rented a garret in the house of John Bell, a rich London merchant who has long dominated his family and his employees by his cruelty and his brutal materialism. His young wife Kitty Bell is in every respect the exact opposite of her lord and master. Whereas he is completely indifferent to everything but his own success, she is acutely alive to the suffering of those around her, and in particular to the unhappiness of the mysterious lodger who has rented the garret. Just as in Eloa, pity turns out to be a synonym for love. The dramatic interest of the play, such as it is, centres upon the unspoken love of Chatterton and Kitty Bell which reveals itself only when Chatterton is dying. He has counted upon the sale of a manuscript to save him from the debtors' prison but the suddenly aroused passion for Kitty Bell engrosses all his faculties and the masterpiece remains unborn. As a last resort Chatterton has written to Beckford, the Lord Mayor, with whom his family had been acquainted, asking for help. Beckford, the conventional official filled with a sense of his own importance and with the rich man's contempt for poverty, descends upon John Bell and demands to see the young poet. He offers him fatherly advice on the subject of putting away childish things like poetry and finally hands him a letter explaining the conditions upon which he will come to his rescue. According to his lights the Lord Mayor has been incredibly generous; he has offered Chatterton a position as first valet de chambre. Human ingenuity could devise no more exquisite insult. Chatterton knows that his creditor is skulking about the house, ready to pounce upon him at the first opportunity. He thinks only of the dishonor that awaits him and he evades it by swallowing poison. His body can be sold to the surgeons to defray the trifling debts that he was unable to pay in life. Luckily the poison works slowly enough to permit the two lovers to reveal their feelings for each other. The only other character of importance is the good Quaker who fulfills the functions of the Greek chorus, aware of the impending tragedy but powerless to avert it. Chatterton expires in his arms, and to the surprise and bewilderment of her husband Kitty Bell dies of a broken heart.

In the final scene Marie Dorval decided to die in a way that the Comédie française considered highly unconventional. During one of the rehearsals a staircase was brought on to the stage. From the top of this staircase which led to Chatterton's room, Marie Dorval announced that she would 'dégringoler.' The idea of this 'dégringolade' convulsed the rest of the company. They could hardly wait to see it, but Marie Dorval refused to give them that pleasure until the first night. Then she would show them how an actress of the Porte St. Martin could die. That day she went to the theatre early, shut herself up in her dressing room and refused to see anybody. The boxes and the orchestra filled up with the usual fashionable crowd from the Faubourg St. Germain, but there was another element in the house for whom Marie Dorval was acting. The parterre was crowded with long-haired pallid young men, unsuccessful poets and artists struggling against starvation, who never sold their works, and who still clung to the belief that there was no other reputable career in the world but poetry and painting. 'Chatterton' was their play, the only play that properly lashed the world for its smug indifference to genius. The climax of the evening came in the melodramatic scene where Kitty

Bell, who had clutched her way up the staircase to Chatterton's room only to find that she was too late and that he had already drunk the poison, collapses against the bannisters and tumbles to the floor. That was the famous 'dégringolade.' The audience sat spell-bound, quivering with emotion. It was the first time that such a thing had been seen in the Comédie française and it was the first as well as the last time in his life that Alfred de Vigny enjoyed a moment of triumph. " Where were you," he wrote to his friend Brizeux, " when all my other friends were clasping me to their bosom." The actors, who had been so consistently opposed to him and to Marie Dorval, capitulated without a word. The success was all the more intoxicating to Vigny in that it was the youth of the nation that was acclaiming him. Maxime Du Camp dated his passion for literature from the first night of ' Chatterton.' Labiche, author of so many rollicking comedies, wrote to Leveaux, one of his collaborators, that his heart was wrung as if it had been clamped in a vice. Berlioz and George Sand were no less enthusiastic. Musset, indignant at the cavillings of a few journalists, rushed to the defence:

> . . . *Messieurs du journalisme,*
> *Quand vous aurez crié sept fois à l'athéisme,*
> *Sept fois au contresens, et sept fois au sophisme,*
> *Vous n'aurez pas prouvé que je n'ai pas pleuré* . . .

In the midst of his triumph Vigny was made utterly miserable by Marie Dorval's flagrant unfaithfulness.

Loyalty and gratitude were words she did not understand. The liaison dragged on for another two years but by the time his mother died, in 1837, it was all over. The relationship had been begun on the loftiest plane of respectful adoration. It ended seven years later on a note of bitterness and disgust. She had betrayed him, she had made him ridiculous to his friends, and she had enticed him into writing at least one letter, which she was careful to preserve, of such extraordinary sensuality that it has never been printed. What she cost him in anguish of spirit cannot possibly be estimated. In return he had treated her with a respect that no other man ever gave her, he had forced the doors of the Comédie française for her, and he had written one play, 'Chatterton,' in which she had reached the high water mark of her career.

Anatole France hints that Vigny's sudden revulsion against her was not the result of her unfaithfulness, which was common knowledge to everybody, but of his discovery in her of a taint of unnatural vice. Certainly that would explain the intensity of his loathing for the whole sex which finds expression in 'La Colère de Samson,' one of the greatest poems he ever wrote but a poem that is curiously foreign to his nature. Here he lifts the veil for a moment and allows us a glimpse of a tortured soul in the nethermost pit of despair.

Une lutte éternelle en tout temps, en tout lieu
Se livre sur la terre, en présence de Dieu,

ALFRED DE VIGNY

Entre la bonté d'Homme et la ruse de Femme,
Car la Femme est un être impur de corps et d'âme.

Throughout the world behold the struggle rage,
God sees its fury still undimmed by age.
Man's truth ever at war with woman's guile,
For woman is a creature foul and vile.

That was the only revenge he allowed himself, and it was not a revenge that could affect Marie Dorval as the poem was not published until long after her death.

Did he remember as he wrote those lines the little book of advice his mother had put into his hands when as a boy of seventeen he had donned the uniform of the Maison du Roi and ridden off to the wars? It had contained one pregnant paragraph about the iniquity of actresses. He may have smiled then at the maternal earnestness of the warning but time had proved it to be strangely prophetic.

CHAPTER VII

L'amour est une bonté sublime.   VIGNY

THE SUCCESS OF 'CHATTERTON,' UNQUESTIONABLE
though it was, aroused distinct opposition in certain
quarters. Realists like Balzac were frankly contemp-
tuous. He summarized the play in three lines — First
Act: Shall I kill myself? Second Act: I should kill myself. Third Act: I do kill myself. Other critics objected
to the play because it seemed to justify or at least to
condone suicide. In the Chamber of Deputies a speech
was actually made condemning 'Chatterton' on that
account and urging that dramatic censorship should
be extended to include morality as well as politics.
The author of this speech, a certain Monsieur Charle-
magne deputy from the Indre, returned to the charge
in the *Revue des Deux Mondes.* Such comments infuriated Vigny's little cohort of admirers who were
equally impatient of Balzac's brutal commonsense
and the extraordinary paternalism of the Chamber
of Deputies. Vigny had suddenly become the spokes-
man of restless youth, the one man of his generation
who had idealized suffering as youth wanted it to be
idealized. To the ardent young romantic of 1835
'Chatterton' was nothing less than the flawless expression of ultimate truth. Thiers, the minister of the

Interior at the time, was inundated with letters from all the unsuccessful poets in Paris threatening to commit suicide unless the State came to their rescue. The twentieth century has no great sympathy with romantic despair but the questions posed by 'Chatterton,' though they have changed their trappings, are still clamoring for an answer. What if anything does society owe to the poet, can genius be subsidized, is it true that sorrow and suffering are more fertile than happiness and success? These are some of the questions suggested by Vigny's romantic drama, and to the public that crowded into the Comédie française on the twelfth of February, 1835, they seemed strangely compelling. One philanthropist at least was so moved by the fate of indigent poets that he founded a consolation prize for them at the Academy — a touching proof of the power of Vigny's emotional appeal. Evidently the tinsel of 'Hernani' had begun to tarnish and the time was ripe for a new kind of romanticism in which there were fewer alarums and excursions and a more incisive moral struggle.

Meanwhile Marie Dorval had given up the rôle of Kitty Bell at the height of her success to play with Mlle. Mars in 'Angelo,' a new play by Victor Hugo. Her subsequent dramatic career was not happy. She drifted from one theatre to another, finding it more and more difficult to get engagements in Paris. Prolonged tours in the provinces, the usual fate of the waning popular actress, and the competition of younger rivals embittered her against her profes-

sion. One last appearance at the Théâtre français in
' Cosima ' by George Sand proved a complete failure.
Domestic troubles also rained down upon her. Ga-
brielle, the daughter who had eloped with Fontaney,
died of tuberculosis. Even more of a blow was the
death of an adored grandchild. In these dark days the
steadying influence in her life was George Sand to
whom she showed a side of her character that Vigny
and her other lovers never suspected. Vigny knew her
as a wayward passionate woman who lived entirely
in her emotions, whereas to George Sand she was primarily a ' brave femme ' working hard and living
without luxury to support an idle husband and three
children. Upon the death of her grandchild she
opened her heart in a letter to George Sand as she
had never opened it to Alfred de Vigny. If Vigny had
only known how she longed for him, how she gave
up her old life and sought consolation in the Bible
and Thomas à Kempis, how in her restless despair
she frequented churches and cemeteries, he might
have felt more charitably towards her. As it was, once
he had broken away from her he never came back.
Two or three years after their separation she wrote
to him asking for permission to play ' La Maréchale
d'Ancre ' to which he replied in a letter of frigid
politeness. As far as we know he never saw her either
on or off the stage during the last seven years of her
life, and he was thus spared her pathetic struggle to
stem the tide of Rachel's rising popularity. In romantic melodrama Marie Dorval was supreme but in
' Phèdre,' which she insisted upon attempting in the

closing years of her life, she was definitely out of her depth.

The end came in 1849 when she was suddenly taken ill on her way to Caen to fulfill an engagement. She was brought back to Paris where she died a few days later. The inscription on her grave in the cemetery at Montparnasse — 'Marie Dorval morte de chagrin' — needs no amplification. In a letter to his cousin, the Vicomtesse de Plessis, Vigny remarked somewhat wistfully that he learned of her death, " as one learns everything nowadays, from the papers." Apparently his cousin had reproved him for his intimacy with an actress. " You must not think," replied Vigny, " that these friendships play so big a part in a man's life as the world thinks," but this assumption of indifference hardly carries conviction. In the very same letter he betrays himself. He admits that he can not bear the idea of seeing any other actress in one of her parts, " for it seems to me when I think of her for whom this was written ' that they are parting her garments and casting lots.' " This spontaneous flash of self-revelation and not the deliberate bitterness of ' La Colère de Samson ' is the real epilogue to the liaison with Marie Dorval. ' La Colère de Samson ' was written shortly after he had broken off his relations with her, when he was still smarting with shame and indignity. Under such conditions a man may speak the truth but it is never the whole truth; that only comes out bit by bit years later when an occasional twinge of pain jogs the memory without distorting it.

During almost the whole period of his intimacy

ALFRED DE VIGNY

with Marie Dorval, Vigny was being racked by domestic worries. His wife had enjoyed uninterrupted ill health since their marriage, and in the year 1833 his mother was stricken by an attack of apoplexy. It was only his unceasing watchfulness that kept her alive for the next four years. Even in Paris it was not always easy to summon a doctor at a moment's notice, and many an evening he would sit by her bedside surrounding her with those little attentions that are often more comforting and more effective than all the remedies of science. Much as he loved her and well as he understood her it was not always an easy task. Her sudden fits of temper usually directed at the mild-mannered Lydia, who with all her faults was a devoted daughter-in-law, left him completely exhausted. The passionate moments he snatched with Marie Dorval were even more disturbing. It was only in the early hours of the morning when he would shut himself up in his room to cover sheets of paper with his fine angular writing — sketches for novels, plays and philosophic poems, most of which were never published — that comparative peace descended upon him.

His mother's death, though in one sense it released him from a burden, accentuated the intolerable loneliness of his life. Neither his wife nor Marie Dorval had the intellect or the insight to enter into the rarefied world of his ideas, and though he had a circle of admiring and sympathetic friends like the Deschamps and Brizeux, he was peculiarly dependent upon the stimulus of women. His mother was the

[133]

anvil upon which he could hammer out his thought. She was also his chief link with the aristocratic world, the monarchy and orthodox Catholicism, and with her death his respect for the great forces of conservatism began to weaken. How much of a part she played in his life, how utterly bereft he was without her we can glean from the journal. The vast literature of confession produced by the romantic movement contains nothing more genuine than Vigny's unadorned narrative of his mother's last illness.

With the death of his mother and his estrangement from Marie Dorval, Vigny was thrown more and more upon the society of his wife. She needed him, and Vigny like any one else enjoyed being needed. It was on her account that he exiled himself from Paris for months at a time and buried himself in the seclusion of Maine Giraud. This little property near Angoulême had been left to him by his aunt, Madame Sophie de Baraudin. He had gone out of his way to pay her a fleeting visit when as an ardent young officer he was en route with his battalion from Strasbourg to the Pyrenees, little thinking that the time would come when he would be living there with an invalid wife. Vigny described his property as a " little fortress surrounded by oaks and elms and green fields and watered by countless springs," but he was never entirely happy in the country. It was only Lydia's child-like enjoyment of nature that reconciled him to it. For him the senseless indifference of nature was almost repulsive, and he far preferred the chimney pots of Paris.

In the month of November, 1838, the placid existence at Maine Giraud, so pleasant to Lydia and so
boring to Vigny, was disturbed by the news of the
death of Lydia's father. Lydia was one of those gentle
Victorian souls, now practically extinct, who have to
be shielded from bad news, but as soon as Vigny
could bring himself to break it to her they started at
once for England. The visit, which lasted some six
months, was not inspired entirely by filial devotion.
Sir Hugh Mills Bunbury, the eccentric millionaire
who could not remember the name of his son-in-law,
had married again and had had several children by his
second marriage. Upon his death it was discovered
that his two older children had been disinherited in
their interest. The will was a cruel shock to the
Vignys who had every right to expect a far more generous treatment. During her father's lifetime Lydia
had received from him £240 a year, and there was
an understanding between them that after his death
if her conduct had pleased him she should be treated
with at least as much generosity as the other children.
In the lawsuit that followed — Vigny would have
liked to settle out of court but that proved impossible
— the Vignys made a great point of the fact that they
had lived on good terms with their father-in-law. Apparently they had some sort of a legal case in that
Lydia and her brother had been born in Demarara,
which having been a Dutch colony still retained the
laws of Holland. Dutch law required an equal divi-
sion of property between the children. The suit
opened in December, 1838, and dragged on for six

years instead of six months which Vigny had fondly hoped would suffice. The law moves in a mysterious way under any conditions, and to a foreigner unfamiliar with the legal machinery but convinced of his rights the dilatoriness of justice was doubly exasperating. Lydia claimed part of the profits in the plantation since the death of her mother, compensation for the money spent by her father on the cultivation of the plantation, and a share in his English property. Eventually the case was compromised. The Vignys renounced all claims upon the estate of the testator in consideration of which they were paid £7500 of which £1500 went to the lawyer. The second wife also agreed to pay £1000 which had been left to the Vignys in a codicil of an earlier will. Roughly speaking, Lydia received what she had always had as an annual allowance from her father. It was not a large fortune, certainly not large enough to justify the sneering comment of Sainte-Beuve — " De Vigny has received a fortune from his father-in-law: it suits him to be rich and it delights his friends — a little gold at the feet of the albatross."

Vigny was frequently discouraged by the slowness of the Court of Chancery but he was philosophical enough to accept the inevitable delays without losing his temper. The course of justice could not be hurried, and in the meantime English society had a good deal to recommend it. There is no place where friends make such a difference as London, and Vigny was particularly fortunate in his English friends. In Paris a stranger can sit outside a café watching the world go by and be vastly entertained, but in London if the stranger is to be preserved from melancholia he must always have the illusion of being at home. Unless he has a club to retreat to he will feel himself an outcast. Luckily his wife's relatives were not all as churlish as his father-in-law. He stayed with them in London, at their house in York Street Portman Square, in Surrey, and at Shavington in Cheshire, and evidently he enjoyed himself in spite of good humored complaints about the cold and the fog. Considering that at home he never opened a window his enjoyment of English countryhouse life is quite remarkable. Shortly after arriving he writes to Buloz, the editor of the *Revue des Deux Mondes,* that " he is being much fêted, but that he is comparatively quiet for the moment because he is surrounded by only six instead of the usual nine children, all of them charming and all of them talking at once."

Certainly Vigny saw the pleasantest side of English life. He was no longer a stranger for he had been in England twice before, once immediately after his marriage and again in 1836. He was at home in English literature, especially in Milton, Byron and Ossian — Europe took an unconscionable time getting over Ossian — and he spoke English fluently though with a strong accent. As a distinguished visitor he was elected a temporary member of the Athenaeum, where he enjoyed that unlimited leisure for reading and study that he had never had at home. " The members do themselves more honor than you in inviting you to join them," wrote one of his English friends.

That was one of those graceful remarks that Vigny himself might have made. John Stuart Mill sang his praises in the ' London and Westminster Review'; ' Servitude et Grandeur ' was adopted at Eton as the book to be studied for the French prize offered by Prince Albert. Meanwhile dinner invitations poured in on him. No wonder that he took kindly to his wife's compatriots.

Unquestionably Vigny was, and still is, one of the French authors whose personality as well as whose writing is wholly sympathetic to the English mind. A better liaison officer between the literary worlds of Paris and London could not be imagined. The Duke of Wellington once remarked that the real trouble with Napoleon was that he did not happen to be a gentleman. That could never have been said about Vigny. No Englishman was more reserved, more jealous of his independence or more aware of his dignity. The Frenchman's effervescent gaiety which is so terribly disturbing to certain kinds of Englishmen was entirely lacking in Alfred de Vigny. At the same time he was a good loser, never railing against fate and never clamoring for sympathy. An Englishman perhaps would never have analyzed his feelings about honor as Vigny does in the journal. "The gentleman or gentilhomme is pre-eminently a man of honor, who out of respect for the decencies of life is restrained within certain limits of behavior which religion would never reach; for certainly there are things that a priest might do which would be quite out of the question for a gentleman." Lord Chesterfield is the only Englishman who could have written those words but thousands would subscribe to the sentiment.

Through the pleasant medium of the Athenaeum, Vigny met the best society that England had to offer. He was introduced by Abraham Hayward, the translator of 'Faust,' a man who is practically forgotten today but whose wit and hospitality were deservedly popular in the early Victorian era. His two articles on gastronomy in the 'Quarterly Review' had brought him considerable celebrity in dinner-giving circles. At the Athenaeum also Vigny may have met Grote and Milman, the two leading historians of the day, but more probably he owed his acquaintance with them to Henry Reeve, the earliest and the most devoted of his English admirers. Henry Reeve was one of the few cosmopolitan Englishmen of his generation. He had been at school in Geneva where he had seen Bonstetten and Sismondi, and he grew up to be as much at home in France and Germany as in England. He contributed to German periodicals, he was an habitué of Madame de Circourt's salon in Paris, and he was on intimate terms with such men as Thiers, Guizot and Lamartine. Later on as a regular contributor to the 'Times' on foreign affairs and as editor of the 'Edinburgh Review' he exercised a wider influence on public opinion in England than some statesmen whose names were far better known. He had already met Vigny on one of his numerous visits to Paris and he had immediately recognized in him a rare spirit, one of those who know how to attune themselves to other people in conversation without losing any of their own savor. On the first night of 'Chatterton' he was among the chosen band who rallied around the author and acclaimed his success. This strangely mature young man of twenty-two was quick to see what Vigny's French admirers ignored, that the play was historically false, and yet he was sensitive enough to appreciate the beauties of the language.

At the time of Vigny's visit to England Reeve was living in lodgings in Grosvenor Place with Henry Fothergill Chorley, an author and a musical critic of some distinction. "We united our efforts," said Reeve "to make our house agreeable. He supplied the music and I part of the society." Judging by the names of their guests, Thackeray, Carlyle, Count d'Orsay, Prince Louis Napoleon, Mendelssohn, and Liszt, the joint efforts were most successful. In this monde Vigny was always welcome. The only one who has left on record an unfavorable impression of him is Carlyle. The solitary reference to Vigny in Carlyle's massive correspondence suggests that they met only once: " The other day I met with a French lionlet, one Comte de Vigny, a Carlist literary dandy, civil, Parisian, with a long Roman nose and next to no chin." Obviously the two men were not likely to relish each other's society. Carlyle would never take the trouble to penetrate the silky politeness of Vigny's manner and discover the stoicism that lay beneath, while Vigny, Anglophile though he was, could hardly

be expected to make the necessary allowances for
Carlyle's dyspepsia.

Vigny had still another contact with English society besides Henry Reeve and the Athenaeum. One
of his oldest friends with whom he had played as a
child at the Pension Hix had long since settled in
England where he had come to be recognized as the
arbiter elegantiarum, 'the most accomplished gentleman of the epoch.' The Count d'Orsay whom Alfred
de Vigny knew was anything but the effeminate dandy
of the Victorian legend. Not only was he a sculptor
of some talent, an author and a brilliant conversation-
alist, but he was also one of the first of the gentleman
athletes: 'the most splendid physical specimen I have
ever seen,' was the comment of N. P. Willis — a man
who excelled in all sports at a time when physical fit-
ness was not as popular an ideal as it is today. He had
married Lord Blessington's daughter, but it was no
secret to anyone but Lord Blessington that he was in
love with his wife's stepmother, the gorgeous Lady
Blessington, with whom he lived happily for eighteen
years. D'Orsay and Lady Blessington are almost the
last example of those long idyllic liaisons of which
the secret seems to have been lost with the increasing
facility of divorce. In spite of Lady Blessington's
equivocal position all the celebrities of the day, literary, political and artistic, instinctively gravitated to
Gore House. Never has there been a salon where intellect and good looks were so evenly divided between
the host and hostess. Lady Blessington was not a blue-

stocking but she was blessed in addition to her beauty
with a certain unaffected cleverness which was quite
sufficient for her purposes. Her book of travels, 'An
Idler in Italy,' contains just the kind of chatter that
the beau monde enjoys. Vigny describes it as a lovely
bouquet fresh from Florence which makes him forget
the smell of English coal. At Gore House he met a
more varied society than the Athenaeum could provide — Lord Lytton, the Disraelis, James Smith of the
Rejected Addresses, Thomas Moore, Macready and
Lord Durham.

It gives some indication of the range of Vigny's interests that the two men who made most impression
on him were these two last, the great actor and the
founder of modern Canada. Vigny always regarded
himself as the unofficial ambassador between France
and England — indeed at one time he cherished hopes
of actually being appointed to the Court of St. James
— and the achievement of Lord Durham in welding
French and English Canada into one nation appealed
strongly to his imagination. Upon the occasion of
Lord Durham's death he wrote a letter of condolence
to Lady Blessington in which he describes him as one
of those rare spirits who belong to the past and the
future at the same time. Durham was the incarnation
of an ideal that was forever beyond Vigny's reach. An
aristocracy of service has always been an exclusively
English ideal. It may be that the world has outgrown
the need for it, but Vigny felt the pull of 'noblesse
oblige' as strongly as the most conscientious peer in
the House of Lords.

ALFRED DE VIGNY

The friendship with Macready was more obvious. Vigny had seen and admired the great actor in Paris ten years before when he was proving to French audiences that Shakespeare was something more than a barbarian. In the autumn of 1838, when Vigny arrived in England, Macready was getting ready to produce Bulwer Lytton's 'Richelieu.' What could be more natural than that he should seek out the author of 'Cinq Mars.' D'Orsay introduced them to each other and they soon became warm friends. From the letters that passed between them it would appear that Macready owed not a little of his success in 'Richelieu' to the vivid details about the life and character of the cardinal supplied by Alfred de Vigny. Their mutual admiration for Shakespeare was another link between them, and as long as Vigny remained in London a box at Covent Garden was always at his disposal whenever Macready was acting.

"How could I not like a country," says Alfred de Vigny, "in which I have been received with such kindness." Other foreigners may have been entertained more extensively but none have met with a more friendly welcome. It is in his letters to women, to the Marquise de la Grange, Mrs. Austen, and Camilla Maunoir, that Vigny's affection for England shows itself most unmistakably. Vigny always revealed himself more openly to women than to men. With his own sex he was inclined to be rigid and too aware of his own dignity but with women he was invariably and unaffectedly charming. The affair with Marie Dorval had cured him of any further desire for passionate liaisons, but a half Platonic, half sentimental relationship with his women correspondents remained a source of constant pleasure. To each in turn he showed a different side of his character. To the Marquise de la Grange, the wife of a former mousquetaire in the Maison du Roi who subsequently made a name for himself as a diplomat and a scholar, his letters are slightly ceremonious but beneath the mask of reserve there is always a certain delicacy of sentiment. It is in a letter to the La Granges that he describes his first sight of Queen Victoria: " The country and the country houses, which people in England like so much in winter and to which I have to go sometimes, are less peaceful than this great Athenaeum which is like a miniature Louvre. The other day the lovely little girl who rules over all this drove past these ancient palaces in her gilt coach without any guard at all, and the populace, if they wanted to, could have lifted the diamond crown off her head. Instead of which they shouted hurrah for Mademoiselle la Reine (I call her that, the Americans call her Miss Kent and Miss Victoria) and they cheered her enthusiastically. You would have liked to see that, madame, you with whom I like to have a little talk too, you who are also a friend at least as far as you have time to be and certainly were a friend, as I shall always remember, when I lost the friend of my whole life."

Vigny's letters to the Marquise de la Grange gradually became less stately in manner but she was too absorbed in her salon and her duties as the wife of a diplomat to offer him any real intimacy. He complains half humorously that friendship only exists in intimacy and that it can never thrive in an atmosphere of fashionable tea parties. More interesting though not perhaps more genuinely affectionate are the letters he writes to Mrs. Austen, wife of John Austen the distinguished jurist. Like her nephew Henry Reeve, Mrs. Austen was almost as much at home on the continent as in England. Auguste Comte said that she was the only woman he knew who was straightforward and intellectual at the same time. She lived in Paris from 1844 to 1848 when she was driven out by her horror of the Revolution. For those four years her house in the rue Lavoisier was the meeting ground for the more intellectual of her compatriots and for such men as Vigny, Guizot and Victor Cousin, some of whose works she translated. Obviously from Vigny's letters she was something of a beguiler besides being an intellectual. " Most assuredly, Madame, it is impossible to find more charming coquetry than that of England as she is represented by you, and there is no paradise one would not abandon with delight for a person who becomes so amiable after succeeding in all her desires. She is exactly like that beautiful lady of the Court of Louis XIV who sent a message to her lover, 'let him understand that I have been unfaithful to him, but I do not bear him any malice.' "

Among the English or rather Irish friends of the Austens was a Mr. Corkran, a correspondent for certain English papers and the father of two daughters, Alice and Henrietta, whom Vigny watched grow up and to whom he became devotedly attached. To Henriette d'Angleterre as he called her Alfred de Vigny was the epitome of romance. While she was still a child he used to kiss her hand and treat her with that elaborate courtesy that always marked his relations with women. Perhaps there was something slightly ridiculous in his clinging to eighteenth century manners, in his long hair tumbling in ringlets about his neck — Lamartine speaks of his 'cheveux ruisselants d'inspiration' — but Henrietta found his society wholly delightful. Sometimes he would take her to the Louvre and show her the pastels of Rosalba, which he wanted her to copy, but more often it was she who decided their amusements. She would consult him about anything that came into her head — the choice of a play for private theatricals or, venturing even further, a costume for a fancy dress ball. Vigny was always at her service, always anxious to surrender to her childish tyranny. Spoiling the children of his friends was a luxury that he never denied himself.

Of all his English friendships there was apparently only one that Vigny owed directly to his wife. Lydia had a cousin Camilla Maunoir, whose father was a native of Angers and whose mother was an English-woman. As soon as he arrived in England Vigny was immediately taken to meet his Anglo-French relations. The meeting must have been successful for Vigny was soon referring to the Maunoirs as a French oasis. Much as he loved England and English ways it was obviously a delight for him to escape occasionally from the Bunbury grandeur of Portman Square to the less pretentious atmosphere of the Maunoirs in St. John's Wood. Camilla Maunoir was a Protestant of great piety, and at the same time a woman of the world without being in the least worldly. There is perhaps just a hint of mockery in the way he addresses her, ' ma chère Puritaine,' and in his insistence upon her gravity and her serious ways, but if so it is the tender affectionate mockery that we reserve for those we love. At one time she seems to have cherished a hope of converting him to Protestantism by introducing him to the works of an eminent Protestant divine of Geneva, but Vigny though he might not accept the dogmas of the Church could never be anything but a Catholic. After he went back to France it was Camilla Maunoir who kept him in touch with affairs in England. She sent him the works of Carlyle as they came out and wrote to him about O'Connell and the Oxford Movement. She also translated some of his poems for his English admirers, which explains perhaps why he discussed his poetry more fully with her than with any of his other correspondents. A literary friendship between a man and a woman is not usually a very hardy growth. It is apt to die of inanition or else to develop into something else. At first glance the correspondence with Camilla Maunoir would seem to be an exception to the rule, but Vigny could never be impersonal in any relationship and his letters to the ' chère Puritaine ' are never merely literary. The popular conception of him as a spiritual hermit living in an ivory tower detached from the rest of the universe is not substantiated by the records of his friendships,

ALFRED DE VIGNY

In spite of the delays and disappointment over the lawsuit the six months that Vigny spent in England were some of the pleasantest of his life, and the scattered references in his writings to English manners and customs and English traits of character are almost invariably complimentary. Where Vigny differs from most foreign observers of the English scene is his readiness to admit a certain delicacy and artistic sensibility in the English people that most travellers consider the peculiar virtue of their own country. After describing the bustle of London, " the symbol of that cold goddess, modern civilization, . . . (the city) where money is God and the Jew banker more than ever Emperor," sentiments which many travellers have echoed since, he concludes with a startling observation: " In the midst of all this activity the arts are neither profaned nor forgotten." Few Frenchmen would even have admitted that there was any art in England in 1840. We are not surprised that Vigny should recognize the traditional virtues of the English people, their business sense and their capacity for government, but it is strange that he should admire them so whole-heartedly. They are not exactly the qualities that we should expect to appeal to a French romantic poet; certainly the English romantic poets were not impressed by them. If Vigny had not been a soldier and a man of the world as well as a poet he would never have been the determined Anglophile that he was. The British Empire represented something for which as a thwarted man of action he could not but have a deep respect. This sympathy with the imperial idea combined with a love of English poetry and the English countryside — he would rather live in Penzance than in any provincial town in France — is more than enough to explain why of all French poets he is the one who understands England the best. His affection for England was not dependent upon his English friends though certainly they added considerably to his enjoyment. It was more fundamental than that. Fortunate as he was in knowing such men as Lord Durham and Macready he was always aware of certain international barriers. " The tremendous efforts made by Frenchmen to establish some warmth, some liveliness in their conversations with English men and women will always be doomed to failure. It is like shooting an arrow at a stone. What the English people lack is the very basis of our national character, quickness of sympathy and a gay imagination."

Only a few foreigners have overcome these barriers. They are not necessarily the most intelligent or the ones who know the country most intimately. They are the few who have arrived at accepting England without taking her to pieces to examine the works. The best example of the twentieth century was Henry James, and of the nineteenth century — Alfred de Vigny.

CHAPTER VIII

*Le pouvoir et la richesse sont deux murailles impé-
nétrables à tous les bruits. Malheur à ceux qui s'y ren-
ferment.*

VIGNY

VIGNY RETURNED TO PARIS IN THE SPRING OF 1839 AND
promptly succumbed to the depression that so often
follows a long holiday. He had some difficulty in explaining to his friends that he had not come back
laden with the wealth of the Indies. Poverty itself may
be easy enough to bear but to remain poor when the
world insists that you have inherited a large fortune
is peculiarly galling. The delay over the lawsuit was
not the only cause of Vigny's depression. For six
months he had been living in a country blessed by a
stable government and presided over by a charming
young queen, a country moreover in which he had
enjoyed the most delightful hospitality and in which
he had been treated with the greatest respect. The
contrast with his own native land could not fail to
impress him. Instead of a stable government he found
a number of noisy orators quarrelling over nothing;
instead of a Queen Victoria universally beloved, a
Louis Philippe beloved by nobody except the carica-
turists who found in him a never failing source of
inspiration.

ALFRED DE VIGNY

As for himself, Vigny found he was still in demand in society but he also discovered that as an author he was losing ground. A literary man can hardly expect to hold his reputation unless he goes on writing, literary popularity being like Shakespeare's Time, 'a fashionable host that lightly shakes the parting guest by the hand and with his arms outstretched as he would fly grasps in the comer.' With the publication of 'Servitude et Grandeur' Vigny retired from the lists of authorship. He continued to write to the day of his death but he published nothing more with the exception of an occasional poem in the *Revue des Deux Mondes*. Some of these poems such as 'La Maison du Berger' and 'La Mort du Loup' have since passed into the language but their spasmodic appearance in a literary journal was ignored by the great mass of the reading public. It is not altogether surprising then that Sainte-Beuve's article 'Dix Ans après en littérature' commemorating the tenth anniversary of the romantic movement should have made no mention of Vigny's name. What is surprising is that Vigny should have felt so bitterly about what he considered Sainte-Beuve's strange lapse of memory that he actually wrote to him demanding an explanation. The critic's reply was cruel, all the more so because it was unanswerable. It must have made Vigny wince with pain. After explaining that he was in the habit of mentioning his friends or not in his articles just as he pleased without being called to account he concludes with a manifesto of the critic's independence. "Believe in my admiration for your talents, in my respect for your noble qualities . . . and in my desire for a complete, savage and well nigh irreconcilable independence."

That any man so self-sufficient and so apparently indifferent to popularity as Alfred de Vigny should have laid himself open to such a rebuff is almost unbelievable but there was a certain justification for his behavior in the literary conventions of the day. There has never been a time when the gentle art of log rolling was more universally practised than in the romantic era. Authors did not hesitate to demand favorable reviews of their books, and even a critic like Sainte-Beuve was not above printing in the appendix to his novel 'Volupté' a private letter from George Sand complimenting him on his literary talents. Vigny was constantly being pestered by his friends to get Buloz to give their works a puff in the *Revue des Deux Mondes*. Victor Hugo was always ready to praise the work of his contemporaries but he expected and received full measure of adulation in return. In writing as he did to Sainte-Beuve, Vigny was not demanding praise so much as justice, and Sainte-Beuve after all was a personal friend, a man who had carefully cultivated his acquaintance and who only a few years before had professed the greatest admiration for his genius.

Vigny considered himself the standard bearer of the romantics. There is hardly a tenet of the creed that he was not the first to profess. He was the first to proclaim the sacred mission of the poet which necessarily isolated him from the rest of mankind. In

' Chatterton' he was the first to give adequate expression to romantic pessimism and despair. The theory cherished by his generation that love justifies all things, that sin can be redeemed by passion, found its first and most persuasive advocate in the angel Eloa. It was Vigny who caught the mantle of Sir Walter Scott, and when we have finished pointing out the absurdities in ' Cinq Mars' it still remains one of the best French historical novels and the only approximation to Waverley. Vigny may not have been a great playwright but ' Othello' opened a breach in the Comédie française for the triumphal entry of ' Hernani,' and in the character of Kitty Bell he created a more realistic romantic heroine than was ever dreamed of by Dumas or Victor Hugo. And yet when Sainte-Beuve came to review the literary achievement of the ten years 1830 to 1840 Vigny was forgotten. Five years' silence had driven his name out of the critic's mind.

It so happened that while Vigny was smarting from Sainte-Beuve's neglect he had the satisfaction of a very pretty compliment from another quarter. One morning the ambassador of Bavaria called upon him with a request from the Crown Prince, afterwards Maximilian II, that he might have the honor of corresponding with Monsieur de Vigny. The Crown Prince of Bavaria was a serious youth with a taste for French literature. He had deliberately picked out Vigny in preference to any one in the Academy as the man most capable of introducing him into the secret of the French genius. Vigny, always jealous of his dignity, agreed to answer any letters that the young man might write to him on the understanding that there was to be no feeling of obligation on his part and no attempt to remunerate him in any way for his services. Less obvious than his pride but still clearly discernible was his gratification at being chosen by a foreign prince as the best possible interpreter of French thought and French literature. At last he was receiving the respect that he had always considered was a poet's due, and he would hardly have been human if the fact that the forty immortals had been overlooked in his favor had not soothed his vanity.

How many letters passed between them is unknown but only one of Vigny's has come to light. This one letter in which Vigny expresses his opinion of his contemporaries shows how generous he could be, unlike Sainte-Beuve, to authors who were personally unsympathetic to him. The Prince had expressed the opinion that with such men as Lamennais, Chateaubriand, and Lamartine, style was everything. They wanted only, as it seemed to him, to amuse and to be picturesque. Armed with the conscious rectitude of youth he reproves them for their lack of high seriousness. Vigny's answer shows how conscientiously he took his task as the Prince's mentor. He had long since outgrown the romantic credo, and except for his assertion of independence and his contempt for pseudo classicism he had little in common with the enthusiasts of 1830. He had detached himself from the group that revolved around Victor Hugo and he had founded a little coterie of his own. For that reason he was all the more anxious to be just to the leaders of the movement that he had forsaken. He insists that each one of the authors whom the Prince criticized had started out on his career with genuine principles and high ideals, and that if these ideals were occasionally lost sight of it was because the passion for pleasing the multitude had intervened. Vigny admired Lamartine as a poet but he could never quite forgive him for being an orator. A contempt for everything savoring of the politician has found its way into ' La Maison du Berger,' one of the loveliest poems in the French language.

Ils sont fiers et hautains dans leur fausse attitude,
Mais le sol tremble aux pieds de ces tribuns romains.
Leurs discours passagers flattent avec étude
La foule qui les presse et qui leur bat des mains;
Toujours renouvelé sous ses étroits portiques,
Ce parterre ne jette aux acteurs politiques
Que des fleurs sans parfums, souvent sans lendemains.

Mistaken are they in their proud disdain,
But the ground quakes beneath these tribunes' feet.
Meanwhile with specious discourses they strain
To please the thronging crowd eager to greet
Their flattery. Soon, true to their traditions,
The crowd salutes these actor politicians
With flowers without perfume, without to-morrow.

A rich civilization always requires the leavening influence of a few men who refuse to accept anything from life unless it is handed to them on a silver platter. Vigny was one of these. Courting popularity, submitting one's destiny to the whim of the populace, was utterly incomprehensible to him. His aristocratic nature shuddered at the very idea. It was not that he posed as a modern Coriolanus exulting in patrician insolence, it was merely that he was possessed with a passion for independence. In 1848 when he was persuaded to offer himself as a candidate for the Chamber of Deputies from the department of the Charente he refused to make any political campaign. He did go so far as to issue a proclamation from Paris stating the facts of his life and offering to devote such qualities as he possessed to the service of his country. The other candidates must have considered his proclamation a model of political ineptitude.

" I shall not come among you to canvass for votes," he assures his constituents. "I shall return to our beautiful Charente only after the verdict has been given. According to my way of thinking the people are in the position of a judge who ought not to allow himself to be solicited, and who ought to be so far respected that no attempt be ever made to influence his decisions.

The judge ought to consider every candidate on his merits. My life and my works are before you.

Alfred de Vigny."

In the next world it may be that the saints are elected to a seat by the great white throne on the strength of just such an appeal but in our present imperfect state candidates for office must be a little more forthcoming. Vigny was overwhelmingly defeated.

ALFRED DE VIGNY

There was only one occasion in his life when he deliberately forced himself to ask for something, and though he finally got it he was bitterly hurt in the process. He wanted to belong to the Academy. It was quite natural that the aristocrat who despised financial and popular success should still hope for some recognition. A seat among the immortals was the only reward that he valued. Unfortunately for Vigny's pride no man can achieve immortality in France unless he applies for it. In February, 1842, it happened that there were two vacancies in the Academy. Vigny presented himself for one of them, and in accordance with the rules of the game he started upon a dreary round of visits soliciting votes. The interview with Royer Collard, a superannuated philosopher who had never heard of Vigny or his works, was the first of the many indignities he suffered. Royer Collard kept him standing in the antechamber, assured him that he had absolutely no chance of election, and then as an afterthought asked what he had written. It appeared that the old man prided himself on having read nothing published within the last thirty years. Vigny marched out of the antechamber without deigning to enlighten him. He was disgusted but not yet discouraged.

The next interview, with Chateaubriand, was slightly more propitious. Chateaubriand admitted that Vigny was the most deserving candidate but he was already pledged to the support of Pasquier, the president of the Chamber of Peers, whose chief claim to a seat in the Academy seems to have been that he had known Madame Chateaubriand for forty years. Visits to other academicians followed but though they promised to vote for Vigny eventually they all had favorite mediocrities who had to be taken care of first. When it came to a vote Pasquier was elected to one vacancy, and Ballanche, an eccentric philosopher who had had the advantage of Chateaubriand's acquaintance for an even longer period, to the other.

The following month there was another vacancy and again Vigny began his weary round of visiting but once more he was defeated by a nonentity. Six times he knocked at the door of the Academy in vain, and it was not until 1845 that he was finally admitted. Other men accepted these delays as inevitable. Vigny took them as a personal insult. Possibly if he had shown a little more deference he might have been elected sooner. Certainly a dash of humor and savoir faire would have spared him considerable mortification. A less inflexible man would have found no difficulty in calling upon the academicians without losing his self-respect but there are always some people — Cordelia was one of them — who find it impossible to humor the world. Vigny wanted to march into the Academy with flags flying. That is not the way the Academy admits its members. Even when he had been elected, in what should have been his hour of triumph, there was further humiliation in store for him.

Vigny's speech of acceptance in which he undertook to point out to his associates the error of their ways fell upon stony ground. The Academy was not accustomed to being addressed in such a pontifical manner. After referring with some emotion to the simplicity of his life and the sobriety of his ambitions Vigny solemnly mounted one of his favorite hobby horses. There are two types of men, he explained to the Academy, which make up the intellectual family. One is the perpetual student, the man who takes refuge in himself, who plans his work to last for all time and carries it out oblivious of his contemporaries. This man, invariably a great writer and usually a poet, is the Thinker. The other type is more concerned with immediate results. He wants to hold office and to direct the course of public opinion. He needs the support and approval of his fellow men. Whether he be a statesman, an orator or a journalist, this man is essentially an Improviser. Who is to decide, continues Vigny, the relative merits of thought and action, but there can have been no question in the mind of the audience that he awarded the palm to the Thinker, the group incidentally to which he belonged himself. Vigny always assumed that statesmen, soldiers, men of action generally were an inferior race of beings, and that the élite of the world was composed of thinkers and poets. The two words were practically synonymous in his mind.

The remainder of the speech was devoted to a eulogy of his predecessor, a dramatist named Etienne, whom he commended in such a way as to suggest a criticism of the other members of the Academy. Etienne had never flattered the man in power whether it were Napoleon or a Bourbon. The inference was perfectly clear; Vigny was determined to follow in his predecessor's footsteps. He had not been reconciled to the July monarchy and he had resisted the pressure that had been brought upon him by certain members of the Academy to make some graceful reference in his address to Louis Philippe. Instead of concluding his speech with the conventional flattery that was expected of him he ignored the King entirely and administered a grave rebuke to the Academy for having been so slow to recognize the modern generation of writers (such as himself), who in the course of the last twenty years had rejuvenated French literature.

The matter of his speech was not calculated to please the audience and the style of delivery antagonized many of those who might have agreed with him. Vigny read it very slowly, distilling every word and stopping to mark every passage where there was a suspicion of applause. When he had finished, the acting director Count Molé rose to reply. The contrast between the two men in appearance, in character and in achievement could not have been more startling.

At the time of his election Vigny was a young looking man of forty-eight. In spite of his magisterial manner there was something perennially ingenuous about the honest expression of his blue eyes. The irreverent might insist that he wore a blond wig made out of his mother's hair, but the general impression of youth and sincerity was not to be denied. Here was a man certainly in whom there was no guile. Not quite a royalist nor yet a republican, an instinctive aristocrat though he had worked hard for his living, he despised everything of which Count Molé was the symbol. Molé was a man of bourgeois antecedents, a time-server who owed everything to Napoleon. He had held various offices under the Empire including the ministry of justice but he was among the first to shift his allegiance to Louis XVIII and he had confirmed his royalism by voting for the death of Marshal Ney. Ambitious, sceptical, and utterly incapable of understanding Vigny's uncompromising idealism, Molé attacked the new academician with more asperity than the occasion warranted. Unfortunately he was the better speaker of the two. At least the Academy preferred their cadaverous looking politician — 'a galvanized skeleton' Vigny called him — with his brusque manners and incisive delivery to the distinguished poet who talked to them very deliberately as if they were rather backward school children.

After paying a perfunctory compliment to Vigny's skill in reproducing the past, Molé attacked him with real animosity for the liberties he had taken with history. Certainly the portraits of Richelieu and Cinq Mars were not historically accurate but Molé was far more incensed by the picture Vigny had drawn of Napoleon in 'La Canne de Jonc.' He happened to single out for his attack one of the most brilliant passages in Vigny's writing and incidentally one of the most convincing descriptions of Napoleon in all fiction. The politician who was so ready to desert the Emperor in 1814 was very generous in the defence of his memory in 1845, all the more so as the Napoleonic cult was just coming into fashion. The legend had sprung Phoenix-like from the ashes recently brought back from St. Helena. Molé ignored the complaint that the Academy had been slow to accept the romantics though he might well have pointed out that the greatest prose writer, Chateaubriand, and three of the greatest poets, Hugo, Lamartine and Vigny himself, had already been elected. Musset followed Vigny into the Academy in 1852. Considering that every one of these was elected before he was fifty years old the Academy can hardly be charged with undue conservatism. Judged by present day standards — the average age of election now is well over sixty — the Academy of 1845 was extraordinarily hospitable to youth.

Vigny's speech and Molé's effective but ill-tempered reply reverberated through the literary world for some time. A faint echo has even reached through the ages down to the novels of Marcel Proust. Madame de Villeparisis in a reminiscent mood mentions the reception of Alfred de Vigny to prove that M. Molé was an homme d'esprit. Vigny considered himself so insulted that he refused to be presented to the King by Molé or even to take his seat in the Academy as long as he was director. Public sentiment was by no means entirely against him. Once again as after the first night of ' Chatterton ' Vigny had the poets on his side. Sainte-Beuve wrote a characteristically feline article damning Vigny with the faintest of faint praise but Hugo and Lamartine instinctively rallied to him. However tedious he may have been, and neither of them heard the speech, there was no mistaking the righteousness of his cause. Poetic solidarity demanded that they should uphold their confrère against the philistine Molé.

It was from Victor Hugo rightly enough that Vigny heard the news of his election, Hugo the friend of his youth whom Sainte-Beuve had tried never quite successfully to estrange from him. Times had changed since they had sat up all night together polishing Dumas' verses while Dumas himself entertained his friends at supper, and the old intimacy had died down, but the flame of friendship was never entirely extinguished. When ' Les Burgraves ' met with an unexpected rebuff Vigny immediately despatched a reassuring note to his dear Victor. " Pay no attention to the Cabal. ' Les Burgraves ' can not fail, it is an immortal work." Such a note was just what the wounded vanity of the poet craved. And when Hugo's daughter Leopoldine was drowned Alfred de Vigny wrote a letter of such real affection to his old friend that the misunderstandings of the past melted away. On this occasion Sainte-Beuve also wrote to the bereaved father, but what a contrast between the two letters of sympathy. Sainte-Beuve seized the opportunity to reproach Victor Hugo for his unfriendliness, though why Hugo should be especially friendly with a man who had been making passionate love to his wife Sainte-Beuve does not explain.

No one was more sensitive than Vigny but he was quite incapable of Sainte-Beuve's cruel egotism. Whatever jealousy there may have been between Victor Hugo and himself he would never have dreamed of referring to it at such a time. Intellectually, it is true, he and Hugo had drifted apart. It was inevitable that a man of Vigny's reflective temperament should be bored by Hugo's rubbish about the 'sainte canaille' and the 'archange révolution,' and no doubt he was slightly embittered by the astounding success of a man whom he knew was in so many ways his inferior. No matter how honestly indifferent we may be to the plaudits of the crowd no one is immune from twinges of jealousy when he catches a glimpse of his friends and contemporaries emerging from their clouds of incense. Victor Hugo was the acknowledged leader of romanticism, and those few friends who refused to worship at his shrine slipped out of his mind all too easily. There was an Olympian selfishness about him which is never quite a stranger to genius. As he stepped from one triumph to another it did not occur to him to take one look back. Like many other successful men he was too busy to keep his friendships in proper repair.

With Madame Victor Hugo Vigny's relations were always cordial and he was an ever welcome, though owing to the ill health of his wife, an irregular, visitor in the Place Royale. In one of her invitations Madame Hugo promises him, to make sure of his acceptance, that he will find only such company as is congenial — "aucun Molé." The rejuvenated friendship was unfortunately cut short by the coup d'état of 1852. Hugo went into exile rather than live in the same country with the man he called Napoleon le Petit, while Vigny captivated by the idea of stability that the new régime appeared to promise became a wholehearted supporter of the Empire. According to Jules Clarétie, an acknowledged Hugo worshipper, Vigny and Montalembert tried to have the author of ' Les Châtiments ' expelled from the Academy for *lèse majesté*. There is no way of disproving this story but as far as we know it is not corroborated by anybody else and it was utterly unlike Vigny to have hounded his friends for their political beliefs.

The differences in political opinion which separated him, this time permanently, from the Hugos were also partly responsible for a slight coolness with Dumas and Lamartine. Dumas is another of the literary men who was driven into exile by the coup d'état of 1852, and like other exiles he rather expected all his friends to follow him. The friendship between Dumas and Vigny dated from the early days of the romantic movement when they were both equally in love, in their different ways, with Marie Dorval. Since then Vigny's taste for solitude had affected their intimacy but the core of friendship remained untouched. "We don't have to see each other," Dumas once said to him, "we read each other's works." On those terms they remained until the day of Vigny's death, and though politics may have once clouded their good relations Dumas was too sensible as well as too good-natured to harbor any ill will. Vigny's grand manner had always mystified and amused him but he knew Vigny well enough to realize that if he chose to remain in France instead of following his friends into exile it was not for any sordid reason of self-interest.

The coolness with Lamartine arose for another reason. Vigny had always conceived of himself as a potential diplomat, and when in 1848 Lamartine became for a short time minister of foreign affairs he hoped to be given the London Embassy. One of his friends, the Comte de Circourt, was appointed to Berlin. Why should not he with his English affiliations be sent to London? Vigny may have forgotten that the provisional government was republican and that in the eyes of the world he was still a legitimist. At any rate the offer never materialized. Lamartine did not last long at the ministry of foreign affairs, and Vigny disconsolate but resigned buried himself in Maine Giraud.

He was never as intimate with Lamartine as he was with Hugo and he seems to have vacillated in his estimate of him between modified admiration and unmodified contempt. His opinion of ' Jocelyn,' ' islands of poetry drowned in oceans of holy water ' is hardly complimentary, but from the letter to Prince Max of Bavaria we gather that Lamartine is the noblest and most genuine of poets. On the other hand no one talks more nonsense than Lamartine, though he is capable of acting intelligently and generously when he gets away from the tribune. The last mention of him in the journal indicates Vigny's real feelings: " I respect every deep passion, I know of none equal to Lamartine's for himself."

These conflicting opinions are not necessarily inconsistent. Lamartine had a certain facility in poetry and in oratory that Vigny theoretically despised.

Actually he coveted it just as an orthodox Jew may despise Gentiles and yet covet certain amenities that Christian society has to offer. Vigny never succeeded in the walk of life that Lamartine found supremely easy. He never swayed an audience and he never wrote highly imaginative histories that flattered the vanity of the people and sold by the thousand. On the other hand he was never reduced as Lamartine was to soliciting subscriptions from his friends for vast literary undertakings that could never be brought to any successful conclusion. Any sacrifice of personal dignity was incomprehensible to him. And yet the over-facile pen of Lamartine has given us a portrait of Vigny that has never been bettered. Certainly the conclusion is exactly what Vigny would have liked to have had said about him: " un grand écrivain, un grand homme de bien, mais surtout le plus gallant homme de siècle."

CHAPTER IX

Le vrai Dieu, le Dieu fort, est le Dieu des idées.

VIGNY

LAMARTINE'S VERDICT HAS BEEN GENERALLY CONFIRMED
by posterity. Even men who would appear to have
little in common with Vigny could not fail to be
impressed by his genius, his honesty, and his incredible air of distinction. To Théophile Gautier,
whose idolatry of Hugo might well have blinded him
to the virtues of one who did not worship at the same
shrine, Vigny was the very incarnation of poetry. To
Flaubert he was one of the few honest writers of the
period. Baudelaire thought him the most generous
of men as well as the noblest of poets. The leading
critic of our own time, Benedetto Croce, considers
him one of the greatest poets France has produced,
and as if that were not enough " probably the greatest
of all French poets of the nineteenth century."
  The typically romantic poetry of his youth written when he was still under the influence of Byron
would hardly seem to justify this praise. It is the
philosophic poems, ' Les Destinées,' belonging to the
last fifteen years of his life, which trickled into print
without causing any immediate sensation, that Croce
must have had in mind when he placed Vigny even

above Victor Hugo in the hierarchy of poets. If all poetry had to be fitted into one of three pigeon holes — imagination, sensibility or thought — there would be no difficulty in selecting the right pigeon hole for Alfred de Vigny. Unquestionably Hugo had a more soaring imagination, Musset was more obviously emotional, but neither of them was interested to the same extent that Vigny was in ideas. Some of these ideas have already forced themselves upon our attention. In ' Moïse,' for instance, in ' Chatterton ' and in ' Stello,' Vigny was forever insisting upon the terrible loneliness of genius. That has always been one of the favorite complaints of the romantic. As he grew older other questions came to occupy his mind and he ceased harping so exclusively on the antagonism of society and genius. By the time we get to the philosophic poems he has fought his way through the slough of despond to the firm ground of stoicism in the face of suffering, and resignation to destiny. This new stoicism finds its highest expression in ' La Mort du Loup,' in which Vigny bows low before the dignity of the stricken wolf. He had already expatiated on the virtues of resignation in ' Servitude et Grandeur Militaires,' but in ' La Mort du Loup ' he goes one step further. The spirit of revolt has passed through every stage of indignation and finally emerged purified by the white heat of silence. The value of silence, proclaimed so vociferously by Carlyle, is supposed to appeal to the Anglo-Saxon rather than the Gallic temperament but it had never found a more eloquent advocate than Alfred de Vigny.

ALFRED DE VIGNY

Hélas! ai-je pensé, malgré ce grand nom d'Hommes,
Que j'ai honte de nous, débiles que nous sommes!
Comment on doit quitter la vie et tous ses maux,
C'est vous qui le savez, sublimes animaux!
A voir ce que l'on fut sur terre et ce qu'on laisse,
Seul le silence est grand; tout le reste est faiblesse.
Ah! je t'ai bien compris, sauvage voyageur,
Et ton dernier regard m'est allé jusqu'au coeur!
Il disait: " Si tu peux, fais que ton âme arrive,
A force de rester studieuse et pensive,
Jusqu'à ce haut degré de stoïque fierté
Où, naissant dans les bois, j'ai tout d'abord monté.
Gémir, pleurer, prier est également lâche.
Fais énergiquement ta longue et lourde tâche,
Dans la voie où le Sort a voulu t'appeler.
Puis après, comme moi, souffre et meurs sans parler."

Alas, despite this lofty word Mankind,
Shame for our weakness dominates my mind!
How one should quit life's round of misery
You, noble beasts, have learned, wiser than we.
That which we were on earth, that which we leave,
Demands our silence; 'tis in vain we grieve.
Ah! traveller wild, full well I know thy ways
My heart was riven by thy dying gaze!
It seemed to say — if that thou canst, then strive
By dint of quiet study to arrive
At this same pinnacle of stoic pride
Where I, the forest-born, mounted and died.
Equally base it is to weep or pray,
Bend to thy weary task without delay,

ALFRED DE VIGNY

In whatsoever field the Fates ordain
Suffer like me, then die with deep disdain.

"It takes the life blood out of me to write a poem like La Mort du Loup," says Vigny in a letter to the Marquis de la Grange, and we can well believe him. The intensity with which he felt everything that he wrote explains, at least in part, his comparative sterility. Anatole France says that the idea of a poem would dwell in Vigny's mind a long time before taking shape and springing into life. Vigny corroborates this theory in the journal when he says that he does not write a book, it writes itself. Unfortunately books do not write themselves, they have to be written. Ideas may be generated without any conscious effort but they float about in the limbo of the mind until they are caught and harnassed and driven into the world between the covers of a book.

What Vigny lacked was the urge to produce, which is characteristic of the greatest writers of every age and country. Careless prodigality may not be a virtue but genius is prodigal and it is very apt to be careless. English literature is all the richer because Shakespeare did not stop to blot a line. Vigny was one of the very few poets of his generation who wrote too exclusively to please himself and not enough to please his contemporaries. Of course there were excellent reasons for his limited output. The continual illness of his wife and of his mother necessitated his acting the role of nurse which is not conducive to the writing of poetry. If Vigny had been a selfish man, a sublime egotist like Shelley, he would not have allowed the cares of family life to interfere with his poetry, but unselfishness was not the only cause of his literary sterility. Vigny's cherished creed of resignation alienated him from the world and paralyzed that capacity for gusto without which the pen drops all too readily from the writer's hand. He was not excited by people nor was he exhilarated by Nature; indeed the cruelty of Nature and her indifference to mankind was one of the facts of the universe that inclined him towards pessimism.

The romantic poet is usually fond of idealizing Nature, of personifying her as a kindly nurse, or at least of regarding her as a harmonious setting arranged for our edification. Vigny would have no truck with any such comfortable sophistry. He was as disillusioned as Hardy and within certain limits even more pessimistic. Hardy seems to consider Nature as in some occult way the accomplice of our successes and failures. The conclusion that we draw from the Wessex drama is that Nature and man share a common fate whereas Vigny, far from feeling any kinship with Nature, is repelled by her cold insensibility. "Never leave me alone with her," he begs, "I know her cruelty far too well." But though Hardy is capable of deriving a bitter satisfaction from the knowledge that all life is rooted in the soil, a satisfaction that was denied to Vigny, he has none of Vigny's faith in the saving grace of ideas. One cannot read 'Tess of the D'Urbervilles' or 'Jude the Obscure' without feeling that as far as the social order is concerned all is for the worst in the worst of all possible worlds. Respectability, marriage, all that the world approves is almost invariably made responsible for the most hideous tragedies. Vigny never approached Hardy's apparent conclusion that man is beaten before he starts. He was so penetrated by the aristocratic ideal that he would have scorned to think that man was powerless of making any headway against fate. The great mass of humanity might be contemptible but there were always the natural leaders, by which Vigny meant poets and thinkers, who could be counted upon to save civilization from disaster. That Vigny was not a thorough pessimist would seem to be proved by his enjoyment of hard work. The pride that comes from making one's own way in the world, the exaltation that follows upon the achievement of a task conscientiously done, were among Vigny's keenest pleasures. A man who is thoroughly convinced of the futility of the universe can hardly find satisfaction in such things.

His favorite character in antiquity was Julian the Apostate in whom thought and action, intellectual honesty and physical courage, were perfectly blended. Julian is the hero of 'Daphne,' Vigny's unfinished novel of which the central idea is the deification of the intelligence. 'Daphne' is really the moral biography of Julian the Apostate. It represents only one third of the book that Vigny meant to write; the other two thirds were to have been devoted to Melancthon and Rousseau. The repeated frustration of the religious reformer always fascinated Vigny, not neces-

sarily because he was a pessimist but because religious reformers are invariably gallant souls fighting
against hopeless odds. Julian appealed to the aristocratic rather than to the pessimistic strain in his
character. No doubt there is an element of courage
in philosophic pessimism that was deeply sympathetic to Vigny. To certain temperaments pessimism
is the postulate of heroism, the necessary stimulus
of conservation and progress. It is only the cowardly
thinkers like Rousseau who impute all the ills of the
world to accident, which prevents Nature from producing spontaneously the complete triumph of reason, justice and goodness, who persist in optimism.
The intellectual courage which dares to envisage a
complete absence of morality and to contemplate the
abyss of misery yawning at our side may well con-
stitute a greater force against evil than blind wilful
optimism.

This particular courage Vigny undoubtedly possessed. He found his one sure refuge against the
bludgeonings of chance not in God and not in Nature but in himself, or as he preferred to put it, in
solitude. This habit of retreating into himself was
often misconstrued by his contemporaries, and the
legend of the ivory tower still suggests a disgruntled
aristocrat indifferent to everything but his own aesthetic well-being and impatient to escape all contact
with his fellow men. There was nothing selfish about
Vigny's love of solitude. As he explains it in the journal it was merely a device for recruiting his energies.
" When I said solitude was holy I did not mean by

solitude separation from other human beings and entire forgetfulness of them, but rather a retreat where the soul can compose itself and exercise its proper faculties and where it can collect all its forces for the production of something great. This production can never be anything but a reflection of impressions acquired in the world, but it will be all the more brilliant if the mirror has been clarified by solitude and purified by the flame of thought and the ardor of hard work."

Vigny's inner life was probably more intense than that of any of his friends. He was too poor to satisfy his craving for travel, and except for the visits to England to look after his wife's affairs he never left his own country. Even a trip to Geneva had to be given up because the modest apartment he had hoped to take for himself and Lydia and a femme de chambre proved too expensive. At the same time he was more aware of the world than some of his globe-trotting friends such as Dumas and Gautier. His interests ranged from the religious vagaries of Lamennais and the doctrines of Saint-Simon to the position of women in modern society and the economic possibilities of railroads. To conceive of him as withdrawing from the world merely to burn with a hard gem-like flame in lonely splendor is to do him the greatest injustice. In many ways, particularly in his attitude towards religion and that strange will o' the wisp we call progress, he was the most modern of his contemporaries. No one has expressed more convincingly the double anguish of our epoch, the yearning

after God and the conviction that the God of established religion is unsatisfactory. His greatest poems,
' Moïse,' ' Eloa,' ' La Maison du Berger,' ' La Mort du
Loup,' ' La Colère de Samson,' the five essential poems
as Paul Bourget calls them, all deal with the loneliness
of the spirit. That certainly is the essential strain in his
poetry but Vigny is more than a philosophic poet.
Philosophy in spite of Milton's tender invocation to
her is intractable stuff for poetry. If Vigny still holds
his own it is not merely because of his stoical philosophy but because he is one of the few poets who
has conceived of woman passionately and intellectually at the same time. Victor Hugo's love poetry is in
comparison mere lyric effusion. Musset may glow
with more passion but it is the passion of adolescence
not of maturity. Only in the poetry of Alfred de
Vigny do we escape from an exclusively romantic
conception of love. In ' La Maison du Berger' the
woman invoked becomes the creature, neither sen-
sual nor divine, from which all beauty emanates.

Que m'importe le jour? que m'importe le monde?
Je dirai qu'ils sont beaux quand tes yeux l'auront
  dit.

The loveliness of the world means nothing to him
until it is translated through her eyes. With all this
fervor of love is mingled the bitter knowledge that
she is a creature of flesh and blood whose beauty will
evaporate in old age or death.

Critics have sought to identify the woman apos-
trophized as Eva in ' La Maison du Berger' with the

mother of the great singer Augusta Holmes. Mrs. Holmes was one of the many women who inspired Vigny with a temporary passion. Jean Gigoux, one of Vigny's artist friends, relates that he appeared at his studio very mysteriously one morning to make an appointment. " I am going to bring you an angel, an Englishwoman, you must make a sketch of her for me. She is leaving Paris and I should like to have some souvenir of her." The angel was apparently Mrs. Holmes. It was during her intimacy with Vigny, after being married for twenty years, that Mrs. Holmes had finally given birth to Augusta, her first and only child. Vigny was chosen as godfather. Scandalmongers insisted that there was a very significant resemblance between Augusta Holmes and the portrait of Vigny painted when he was a young mousquetaire, but however that may be the figure of Eva is so shadowy that there is nothing to indicate that the poet had any particular woman in mind when he wrote ' La Maison du Berger.' Eva is the incarnation of all tenderness, an idealized conception of what Marie Dorval should have been and was not.

' La Maison du Berger ' corrects the intense pessimism of ' La Colère de Samson ' written a few years earlier when Vigny was still smarting from the flagrant infidelities of Marie Dorval. In that poem Vigny had plumbed the depths of despair. The heart that is disillusioned and yet can not cure itself of love is surely the most tragic of all themes. Vigny's Samson abandons himself to ignominy with eyes open because he can not fight against his lower nature. Unquestionably the poem is autobiographical but it does not represent by any means the whole truth about Vigny. He was too fond of women to cherish a perpetually insensate hatred of them, and 'La Maison du Berger' confirms what we knew already from the Journal, that he emerged scarred but not shattered from the shadows of misogyny.

Vigny's impatience with politicians, another strand of thought in this curiously variegated poem, has already been mentioned but there is still another element which distinguishes it from the great mass of romantic poetry of the period. The conventional picture of two lovers weary of civilization seeking happiness in the caravan of a peasant changes abruptly into a most unexpected invocation of the spirit of progress. In the middle of the nineteenth century progress meant railroad development. The two lovers may flee from the haunts of men but they can not escape the relentless iron rails that year by year are linking humanity closer.

Mais il faut triompher de temps et de l'espace,
Arriver ou mourir.

The spirit of the twentieth century, the passion for quick communication regardless of what we have to communicate, has never been expressed more concisely. Today we are considering whether we can domesticate the radio and make it a good servant instead of a tyrannical master. In 1842 Vigny was speculating in the same way about the potentiality of the railway for human happiness. A serious acci-

dent on the new Versailles railway in which fifty-
seven persons were killed had caused an outcry
against the " smoking iron bull " that man had called
into being without knowing how to control. Throughout the 'thirties there was considerable discussion in
the Chamber over railways. Even as late as 1840
Thiers, convinced that they were useless for long
distances, had advocated a maximum construction
of thirty miles a year. He insisted that the railway was
only a plaything for children and Parisian pleasure
seekers. Vigny knew better. He deplored the inevitable struggle between man and machinery but
though he foresaw new catastrophes he was not discouraged. Nor was he deceived into thinking that
industrial progress necessarily generated human happiness. Once again he took refuge in his impregnable stoicism. It is true that the steam engine has
come to stay and that distance and time have been
vanquished, but as a result of the victory the fra-
grant charm of travel has evaporated. Though it is
no use holding back the hands of the clock we need
not pretend that the new order brings the millennium
in its wake.

The philosophic poems are all part of one continu-
ous effort to strip life of its sophistries and to contemplate the problems of the world dispassionately. Only
in ' La Colère de Samson ' did his iron restraint give
way. Sainte-Beuve, who understood his foibles without apprehending his greatness, complains that
Vigny's imagination and his intelligence were always
at war with each other. As a philosopher he was at-

tracted by the idea of progress, and yet he hated
every manifestation of the new order. He wanted to
be a dramatic poet but in spite of the success of
'Chatterton' he recoiled from any further contact
with the theatre. 'Moïse' and 'Eloa' are two of the
most fervently religious poems in the language, but
Vigny himself, says Sainte-Beuve, had no more religion than Voltaire. Such criticism assumes that rigid
consistency is a necessary attribute of genius whereas
we know that every thinking man is continually being
forced into inconsistencies.

One of the hallmarks of romantic poetry is its
persistent interrogation of the universe. What do we
mean by God or by Nature? What obligations to
each other do we recognize? The varying answers to
these questions depends upon the mood and the age
of the poet. The difference between Vigny and his
contemporaries is that he tried to arrive at some conclusion by a process of thought instead of subjecting
his intellect to his emotions. All of his great poems
were pondered for years before they saw the light.
They were bred in the brain rather than in the heart.
The quality of inspiration which played so great a
part in the genius of Victor Hugo was practically denied to Vigny. Certainly he was inconsistent in that
in one poem he wrote of woman as if she were an un-
clean animal, and at the same time he treated every
woman he met with the most perfect courtesy, but
only a maniac would try to make his behavior coin-
cide with the ideas expressed in 'La Colère de
Samson.'

To argue that he had no more religion than Voltaire, presumably because for the greater part of his life he was not a practising Catholic, is equally misleading. All his life he was yearning after God and the yearning was none the less genuine if he found the God of established religion profoundly unsatisfactory. The fact that the Almighty could tolerate so much unmerited suffering made him rebellious, but he never in his darkest moments denied God nor did he ever take refuge in the petulant blasphemy that some of the later romantics seemed to have found comforting. Romanticism and Catholicism involving as they do the revolt and submission of the individual will always be hard to reconcile. Vigny was emphatically a romantic in that he believed that it was man's duty to struggle against destiny. Prometheus and the Satan of 'Paradise Lost' were the patron saints of his generation. Only in so far as he resented the existence of evil can he be called anti-religious. In 'Le Mont des Oliviers' he depicts Christ in the garden of Gethsemane pleading with God to obliterate from the world the two monsters, Doubt and Evil, but God's only answer to the prayer is inscrutable silence.

Vigny must have known that his narrowly intellectual approach to the most insoluble problem of the universe was peculiar to himself. Like many unbelievers he acknowledged the stabilizing force of Catholicism and he welcomed it for the country at large. He believed in the saving grace of ecclesiastical conventions and on his deathbed he made his peace with the church and gladly accepted the last rites.

But for the greater part of his life from the time he was a young mousquetaire down to his last illness he fell back for his salvation on heroic pessimism, the bitterest anodyne the mind of man has ever conceived for his consolation. To go through life without hope and without fear, to evolve a certain code of behavior for oneself without expecting any reward human or divine other than one's own self-respect, may be fortifying but unless a man be made of granite it is not conducive to gaiety or even peace of mind. Vigny is one of the rare instances of a man who had discarded all faith in a beneficent deity, all hope of happiness in this world or the next, and yet had managed to keep untarnished his love for humanity. He was not one of those who go about professing philanthropy and the brotherhood of man. Not for a moment did he fool himself into thinking that it was easy to adore humanity *en masse,* but no one reacted more instinctively to the spectacle of suffering.

On one occasion the plight of an impoverished Oriental scholar named Desgranges was brought to his attention. Desgranges was an old man who had given thirty years of his life to the study of sanskrit. Finally he presented the manuscript of his grammar to the ministry of education. He hoped to have it published by the Royal Printing Press which happened to be the only press in the country that possessed sanskrit characters. For eleven years they kept putting him off with one excuse after another. During those eleven years his wife went insane and his daughter committed suicide. Vigny befriended the old man, pleaded his case at the ministry of education and finally after another year's delay got the grammar printed. Desgranges was rewarded for his martyrdom by the pleasure of correcting the proofs. A few days after the publication of his beloved grammar he died. It was the old story, so popular with the romantics, of genius left to starve by the roadside while officialdom passed by on the other side. To bring some happiness into the life of a starving poet or scholar gave Vigny more pleasure than any literary triumph of his own. " L'amour est une bonté sublime," he writes in the Journal, and unlike some philanthropists he meant what he said.

Apart from his religion of love the only faith that Vigny cherished was a belief in the supremacy of ideas. " Le vrai Dieu, le Dieu fort est le Dieu des idées." Somehow or other, in spite of the blundering stupidity of humanity, knowledge, wisdom, intellectual curiosity, whatever we choose to call it, will ultimately prevail. ' La Bouteille à la Mer,' the poem in which Vigny expresses this idea with most conviction, refutes once again the theory that Vigny never escaped or even wanted to escape from the castle of Giant Despair. Because he hugged no delusions about happiness it does not follow at all that he denied the necessity of struggling against fate. Any man who believes as profoundly as did Vigny in the value of effort can hardly be a thoroughgoing pessimist. In ' La Bouteille à la Mer ' Vigny pays a tribute to the spirit of science. The ship of an explorer has been wrecked and God has allowed every member of the crew to be drowned. But though life is thus wantonly destroyed by an insensate Deity thought is not obliterated. The frail bottle containing scientific data of inestimable value to humanity comes safe to land. However feeble a creature man may be and however easily crushed by the universe there is always something in him, his capacity for thought and for perpetuating his ideas, that can never be extinguished.

Vigny's poetry is so obviously the fruit of meditation rather than of emotional experience that it requires some effort to remember that the author of ' Les Destinées ' was not a disembodied intellect but a singularly vivid personality. The events of Vigny's life played only a small part in his biography. It contains no wistful recollections of childhood such as we find in Victor Hugo or Lamartine. Occasionally, as in ' L'Esprit Pur,' the last and most self-revealing of his poems, we catch a glimpse of the gentleman, the aristocrat basking in the halo of his ancestors, but almost immediately the gentleman fades into the agnostic poet who surveys his ancestors with affectionate condescension. The ' vieux noms inutiles ' of those war-loving, boar-chasing country squires will be buried in oblivion while the name of their poet descendant who has dedicated himself to a life of the spirit will be remembered forever.

Just how far it is possible to understand the poetry of another nation will always be questionable. There are certain qualities in Racine, for instance, that the

foreigner can never hope to appreciate. However profound his knowledge of the language there are ca-
dences in the Alexandrine line that can never convey
the same pleasure to him as they do to a Frenchman.
Thanks to Lytton Strachey's essay the foreigner can
no longer accuse Racine of being an empty rhetori-
cian but even Lytton Strachey can not compel enjoyment. He can only indicate the riches of the promised
land that the great majority of us can never hope
to enter. The gulf that separates us from Alfred de
Vigny is not nearly so impassable. Whether we get
the same pleasure from him as a Frenchman is very
doubtful but no two people get the same pleasure
from poetry and it is not important that they should.
It is at least equally doubtful whether we are instinctively aware of an occasional awkwardness in his
verse resulting from his habit of loading every stanza
with almost more freight than it can carry. It may be
that the magic quality of incantation, the perfect
blending of thought, feeling and expression such as
we find in Keats' Odes, is not characteristic of Vigny
but few foreigners are sufficiently familiar with the
French language to sense the absence of this flawless
perfection.

Vigny excels as a poet in the expression of ideas,
and ideas evade the barriers of language more readily
than sentiments. It is always easier to penetrate a
man's thoughts than his feelings. Some of Vigny's
ideas were vigorously challenged by his own generation and they have not been wholly accepted by ours,

but he is one of the few poets of his generation who does not seem to be living in a different intellectual world from ourselves. Vigny's God, 'le Dieu fort, le Dieu des idées,' is a deity the twentieth century can understand.

CHAPTER X

Qu'est-ce qu'une grande vie, sinon une pensée de la jeunesse exécutée par l'âge mûr?

VIGNY

THE LAST TWENTY-FIVE YEARS OF VIGNY'S LIFE WERE years of intense intellectual activity of which, so far as posterity is concerned, one slim volume containing eleven philosophic poems is the only result. The literary man who is perpetually writing without publishing anything is always a ridiculous figure to his more prolific brethren. Sainte-Beuve, who at one period of his life produced a *causerie* a week for five years with unbroken regularity, could never bring himself to believe that Vigny was writing anything at all. Camilla Maunoir, the 'chère Puritaine' with whom he had made such friends in England, accused him of devouring his children like Saturn. There was some truth in the accusation for Vigny was very apt to destroy his literary offspring. He held such an exalted view of the dignity of letters that it was not easy for him to appear in print. And yet Vigny was not one of those flawless artists like Heredia whose every sonnet glows with conscious perfection. There have been many poets who polished their verse with more care. It was always the development of the idea

rather than the actual expression of it that he found
so arduous, and if the idea did not develop the poem
or the novel in which it was to have been enshrined
was mercilessly destroyed.

Vigny's apparently unruffled life was very decep-
tive. To his fellow academicians he was a dignified
poet who had been outstripped by his contemporaries, a sincere artist no doubt but a little too impressed with his own importance. In the Faubourg
St. Germain he was regarded as a charming eccentric.
His letters to the Marquise de la Grange and the
Duchesse de Maillé may affect to despise the chatter
of the salon but he had inherited too much of the
ancien régime to be really indifferent to the charm of
good society. Madame d'Agoult who consoled herself
for the prolonged absences of Liszt by attracting everybody who was anybody in literature or politics to
her door found no one more sympathetic than Alfred
de Vigny. He wrote poetic letters to her about her
crystal soul, and he talked to her eloquently and end-
lessly about Marie Dorval. Probably she never suspected that these confidences were a form of
recreation, and that the genuine Vigny was leading
an intense intellectual life which neither she nor
Marie Dorval would ever share.

A more intimate friend was Louise Colet, the
mistress of Flaubert. She was a determined woman
with a certain facility in poetry and an extraordinary
capacity for choosing her lovers from among the most
distinguished men of the day. The list includes
Victor Cousin the most celebrated philosopher, Al-

fred de Musset the tenderest poet, Flaubert the greatest novelist, Babinet the cleverest doctor, and incidentally Alfred de Vigny. She wrote endless volumes
of poetry, four of which were crowned by the Académie Française thanks to the good offices of Victor
Cousin. Her appetite for fame was insatiable and fame
of a certain kind she achieved, though it was not exactly the fame she sought. If her name still survives it
is because of Flaubert's letters to her and because of
an epigram of Alphonse Karr whom she stabbed in
the back rather clumsily for suggesting that the father
of the child she was about to bring into the world was
Victor Cousin. Alphonse Karr had the knife framed
and under it wrote the inscription: ' Offert par Mme.
Louise Colet . . . dans le dos.'

Her relations with Alfred de Vigny were less tem-
pestuous than those with her other lovers. They were
on terms of friendship for eight years during which
time he wrote her a number of affectionate letters.
It was characteristic of their feeling for each other
that he talked to her a great deal about the business
of the Academy and about his wife's health. Their
liaison appears to have been broken off about the
year 1854, not by any scene but by mutual consent.

Vigny disclosed still another side of his character
to the peasants of Maine Giraud. In Paris he was
always the man of letters but at Maine Giraud,
the property in the Charente that had been left
to him by his aunt Mme. Sophie de Baraudin, he
was primarily the gentleman farmer. As soon as he
moved to the country the fact that he happened to

be a poet and an academician became of secondary
importance. Vigny always insisted that he did not
like the country. He could write eloquently about
the feudal castle of his ancestors and the magnificent
oaks and elms that surrounded it but the charm of a
lovely countryside was a poor substitute for the
chimney pots of Paris. For many years his visits to
Maine Giraud were as brief and as infrequent as possible. He complained that his property was like a horse
which one boards at great expense and only rides once
every seven years. It was not until after the Revolution of 1848 when he spent the greater part of three
consecutive years at Maine Giraud that he began to
interest himself in the life of the community. Lydia
had all the Englishwoman's traditional love of the
country, and the air of Maine Giraud agreed with
her better than the air of Paris. Vigny resigned himself to a bucolic existence and soon discovered that
it had its compensations.

He began by unconsciously magnifying his charming little property until the unpretending manor
house bought by his Baraudin grandfather in 1768
was transformed into a feudal castle that had been
in the possession of his ancestors for four hundred
years. He speaks wistfully of the long deserted halls,
which never existed except in his imagination. In the
same way in the course of an interview with Louis
Philippe he refers to his grandfather as an admiral
who had played a distinguished part in the naval
battle of Ouessant. The Marquis de Baraudin had
enjoyed a reputable though not particularly distin-

guished part in the navy, but he was never an admiral
and he was not present at the battle of Ouessant.
Vigny's genealogical inaccuracies need not be regarded as a reflection on his honesty. As a child he
had probably heard stories about the feats of his ancestors and he never troubled himself to verify them.
Numerous old parchments and family records had
been stored away at Maine Giraud for years. Doubtless they were difficult to decipher but a casual glance
may well have led him to conclude that his bellicose
forefathers played a more important part in national
history than they actually did. After all it is only
very recently that such peccadilloes as errors in
family history have been elevated to the rank of
cardinal sins. In many ways our social code today is
much more easy-going, but tampering with the genealogical tree happens to be one of the vices that
we feel more strongly about than our forefathers.

The next step after investing Maine Giraud with
an aroma of romance was to cast himself in the rôle
of the benevolent overlord. Little by little Vigny began to busy himself with the estate. At first he confined himself to making a garden for Lydia. The
avenue leading to the house was planted with lilac
and clematis. Lydia is afraid of thunderstorms so the
old manor must immediately be equipped with modern lightning conductors. Maine Giraud was the one
place in the world where Lydia was comparatively
well and happy so it must be made as delectable for
her as possible. Where her comfort was concerned no
detail was omitted. He still lamented that he was

never free and that the illness of his wife confined
him to the solitude of Maine Giraud but imperceptibly he found himself getting absorbed in the life of
the countryside. He began by employing local workmen to undertake the necessary repairs to the parquet
floors and the panelling, which they did willingly and
vigorously but without much skill. When he had
spent as much as he could afford on Maine Giraud
and on helping the peasants to repair their own
houses he busied himself with the problems of farm-
ing and wine growing. The Charente is one of the
best districts in France for the production of cognac,
and M. Alfred de Vigny the poet philosopher had
very definite ideas on the proper methods of distilling
brandy. For 'burning' his eaux-de-fie he prefers
wood to peat. No professional vigneron could be
more pleased when he learns that his cognacs have
the reputation of being the purest on the market,
and he is delighted when he can tell his agent that
Hennessey, then as now one of the great brandy
houses of the world, has promised to pay him the
very top price.

Lydia was too much of an invalid to be of any help
to him in the business of the estate. Occasionally she
might stroll with him through the fields and vineyards
near the house but more often he would stride over
his little feudal domain alone. The peasants soon became accustomed to the tall pale gentleman always
dressed in a long black coat and a top hat who greeted
them with such courtesy and seemed so much interested in their affairs. When the day's work was over

he liked to stop in at their cottages to watch them dancing or to listen to their singing of old-fashioned songs. In the middle of the nineteenth century the patriarchal instinct was not yet an anachronism. Sometimes of a Sunday evening especially in winter Vigny would gather the servants in the dining-room and read to them or join them in what must surely have been a rather solemn game of cards. If oral tradition is to be trusted there was not one of them that did not adore him. Decidedly Vigny the country gentleman was more popular than Vigny the academician.

Feudal as his relationship was with the peasants of the neighborhood it was an enlightened feudalism that realized the growing importance of education. He tries though without success to establish a public library in the neighboring village of Blanzac. When he is back in Paris he writes to his agent at Maine Giraud to find out the number of children who have reached school age. With that information in his pocket he calls on the minister of education and insists, this time successfully, on a school teacher for his commune. The subject of education was always very dear to his heart. It was not enough that the peasants should learn to read and write correctly. If they were to vote intelligently they must become civilized and the only road to civilization lay through the broad domain of the French classics. He was even willing to waive the familiar routine of Latin and Greek provided Corneille and Racine were not neglected. He would like the school children to act plays with a view to learning to speak their own language more readily, and with some difficulty ' Esther ' was finally produced. The problem of costumes presented some difficulties but Vigny succeeded in borrowing everything that was necessary from the theatre at Angoulême.

There is a touch of pathos in the picture of Alfred de Vigny setting forth on a crusade to raise the level of intelligence in the Charente and ending up borrowing purple cloaks and cardboard crowns for a village Esther. Vigny's fellow academicians might have smiled at the thought of their dignified colleague coaching the schoolchildren of Blanzac for their prize day performance but such humble tasks as these had always occupied the bulk of his time. At Maine Giraud the greater part of his life was devoted to the most mundane tasks. The whole business of the household fell on his shoulders. A bundle of letters to his agent that have only recently come to light indicate the kind of problem that engaged his attention. Judging from this correspondence the historian of rural economy has more to learn from Vigny than the student of literature. He attended to everything — the supply of dusters, white woollen stockings for the servants, the weaving of linen sheets, the proper packing and marketing of peaches and pears, the regular airing of pillows, bolsters and mattresses, and the everlasting war against rats.

Was ever poet more completely immersed in the prosaic details of life? In one letter he inquires anxiously how Lydia's parrot is standing the recent cold spell and when he discovers that the poor bird has succumbed he issues the most careful instructions for the preservation of the remains. " I am really distressed to hear of the parrot's death for Mme. de Vigny was very fond of it. Are you sure that no one was stupid enough to give it parsley, which is fatal to parrots, or that it was not wounded by cats . . . Find out from M. Lafont at Blanzac if he knows any one at Angoulême who understands the art of taxidermy . . . If it is too late to think of stuffing and if the plumage is still in good condition I should like you to pluck all the feathers and put them in a box so that they may be preserved. They were the great beauty and the only merit of the poor bird." Apparently the beloved bird was preserved, at least a slightly mangy stuffed parrot is still exhibited at Blanzac, which is said to have been the property of Madame de Vigny.

If any husband ever made amends for unfaithfulness it was Alfred de Vigny. Not only did he nurse his wife through every illness but he brushed every pebble from her path. Romantic love he could not give her but whatever happiness comes to a woman from affectionate companionship and from unremitting attention to her comfort was hers. Lydia always came first. After Lydia's slightest whim had been satisfied the business of Maine Giraud and the welfare of his peasants claimed his attention. Vigny would never have dreamed of neglecting his responsibilities. He gloried in all the petty obligations that a conscientious landlord deliberately incurs. It was only when the day's work was over and when every one else was in bed that he allowed himself to indulge in a debauch of study and contemplation.

Maine Giraud is far from being the rugged feudal castle of Vigny's imagination. It stands in a hollow surrounded by vineyards and smiling fields of corn, a pleasant *manoir* but hardly a fortress. Of the great forest that used to extend up to the courtyard nothing remains but a few oak trees. The first thing that strikes the eye is a tower about forty feet high surmounted by a weather vane bearing the initials A. V. The date 1464, which is barely legible, explains the dilapidated condition of the walls. In a monastic cell at the top of this tower Vigny found a sanctuary from the insistent clamor of the world. Here in the small hours of the night he would shuffle off the worries of the gentleman farmer and hark back to the things of the spirit. A chair, a small desk, a mattress in an embrasure in the wall, and a chest containing his manuscripts, were all that his austerity demanded. From the narrow slit of a window he could look down upon the courtyard and catch a glimpse of the vines and the waving corn beyond. Such was the grim little study which posterity has transformed into an ivory tower.

It was here that he wrote the lines describing the mute agony of the dying wolf, here that he pondered over his books of philosophy, and that he conceived of various extensive literary undertakings none of which were destined to be finished. One of these was a historical romance commemorating the history of

Blanzac, which was taken by the English and later recaptured by the French in the Hundred Years' War. Perhaps Vigny hoped to find in the local records some mention of the prowess of his ancestors but if so he was disappointed. Another historical romance which promised better things was sacrificed to his political ambitions.

Vigny's defeat at the polls in 1848 and 1849 had not cured him of a longing to play some part in directing the course of national events. The short-lived republic of 1848 had proved a disappointment. Vigny was not able to convince anybody of his republican sympathies. The sudden rise to power of Napoleon III seemed to offer a new opportunity. He had met Prince Louis Napoleon, as he then was, at Lady Blessington's and at various other houses in London. Fifteen years later when the Prince President happened to be passing through Angoulême he invited Vigny to an official dinner to meet him. Vigny went and was delighted to find the Prince just as simple, friendly, even affectionate in manner, as he had been in London. The only effect of success had been to make him somewhat melancholy. The Prefect of the Charente was so struck by their long intimate conversation that he began to wonder whether it was he or Alfred de Vigny who was receiving the Prince President. Vigny has left no record of what took place during the interview but evidently he expected some tempting offer to be made to him. The Empire was the first régime to which he had rallied with a whole heart. The Coup d'Etat of 1852, by means of which

Louis Napoleon sloughed off the presidency and became Emperor Napoleon III, did not alienate him as it did so many of his friends.

Vigny was not a doctrinaire republican and whatever love he may once have had for the monarchy had long since died of inanition. He could never forgive Louis XVIII and Charles X for not singling him out for promotion. His relations with the Bourbons, he notes in the journal, were like those of a faithful wife to a husband whom she has ceased to love. As for the house of Orléans he had always considered Louis Philippe a usurper and a timid apologetic usurper at that. On the other hand the new régime of Napoleon III promised well. In the early 'fifties Vigny believed and not unnaturally that the Empire meant peace and prosperity and that Napoleon was the one man capable of giving France an efficient and enlightened government. He is tremendously impressed by the results of the plebiscite and he urges his friends to teach their children to sing Vivat l'Imperator. Fortunately he did not live long enough to see that the efficiency and the enlightenment were limited to surface decoration. The Boulevard Haussman and the International Exhibition were hardly sufficient to compensate for the truculent and eventually disastrous foreign policy.

Whatever promises Napoleon may have made to Vigny in the course of their interview at Angoulême never materialized. The rosette of the Legion of Honor and an invitation to Compiègne, which had no sequel, were the only manifestations of Imperial favor. Vigny would have liked to be appointed tutor to the Prince Imperial. His correspondence with Prince Maximilian of Bavaria and the letters he received from admiring young poets had persuaded him that he had a talent for fashioning the taste and the character of the younger generation. There was indeed a guileless quality about him, a complete sincerity and disinterestedness that youth always finds endearing, but he was not one of those rare spirits who attract good fortune without seeking it.

Once again Vigny's inflexibility barred the way to worldly success. So great was his horror of toadying that he became almost a hypocrite reversed. As soon as one of his friends obtained a political position Vigny made a point of dropping him. Unless the successful friend were very insistent they inevitably drifted apart. Vigny could have had a pension if he had been willing to flatter Louis Philippe, and if he could have brought himself to write a cantata in honor of the Prince Imperial as requested by Persigny, the Emperor's secretary, Napoleon would probably have remembered his promises. But the idea of writing panegyrics was abhorrent to him. Instinctively he shied away wherever he suspected that he was being hired to bolster up authority. He wrote only to please himself, never to curry favor with the great. The only concession to ambition that he made was to give up a novel which might have wounded the susceptibilities of the Army. The extraordinary facility with which generals transferred their allegiance from Bourbons to Bonapartes was hardly a happy subject for an author who had ostensibly rallied to the Empire. Considering that Vigny had lost the faculty or the desire of writing for publication the abandonment of the novel was no great sacrifice.

Vigny's hopes were so repeatedly frustrated that his failure to secure a position through his acquaintance with Napoleon III can hardly have been very disturbing. After all, the cloistered seclusion of Maine Giraud offered a richer life than the tinsel grandeur of the Court. As a young man he was often afflicted by ennui, the disease that devastated so many of his contemporaries, but as he grows older the references to ' *la grande maladie de la vie* ' are less frequent, and once he was settled at Maine Giraud he was far too busy to give way to the luxury of boredom. The man who lives by intellect alone is always more likely to be impressed by the futility of existence than the man who works with his hands. At Maine Giraud Vigny was close enough to the soil to catch something of the inherent sanity of agricultural life. The hardheaded ' vignoble ' who produced the best cognac in the Charente had no inclination to brood over the pointlessness of human effort. At the same time Vigny's literary friends kept him in touch with the great world of Paris. The most faithful of his correspondents in these later years was Philippe Busoni, the literary critic of the ' Illustration ' and the author of a volume of poems ' Les Etrusques,' which recalls the concise impersonal quality of ' Moïse ' and ' Les Destinées.'

Busoni was one of the group of minor poets includ-

ing Barbier and Brizeux who had followed the standard of Alfred de Vigny instead of joining the great
army of admirers with which Victor Hugo had surrounded himself. He is the one man who understands
all of Vigny's moods. He can regale him with the gossip
of the theatre, he can listen sympathetically to Vigny's
ingenuous plans for the civilization of Blanzac, and to
the saga of Lydia's unending succession of illness and
convalescence. More than anything else it was the
news of the theatre that Vigny wanted to hear. Was
it true that Rachel had been seen studying the part of
Desdemona in his translation of ' Othello ' ? Why had
Madame de Girardin insisted on giving Judith, in her
play on Judith and Holofernes, as many virtues as
Rachel had lovers? These are the sort of questions
that Busoni has to answer. In particular Vigny wants
to know what sort of person was the young actress
who was being considered for Kitty Bell in the pro-
jected revival of ' Chatterton '? Apparently Mlle. Rose
Chéri had made a great success in ' Quitte pour la
Peur,' the little comedy that Vigny had written for
Marie Dorval. The idea of anybody else playing Marie
Dorval's parts was not easy to stomach but Busoni
must see her and report on her performance. It was
always difficult to revive Vigny's plays for no dramatist was more fussy about the cast. For a long time Ar-
séne Houssaye had hopes of producing ' Chatterton '
and ' Othello ' but Vigny was so difficult to please that
Houssaye soon realized that he was only wasting his
time.

Next to the theatre the business of the Academy

was nearest to Vigny's heart. When he was elected president as successor to Molé he hurried back from the country, somewhat to the surprise of his friends, to take up his new duties. No doubt he felt that belated justice was being done to him. He who had been publicly insulted at the time of his reception was now in a proud position of authority. It was pleasant to preside at meetings of the greatest academy in the world and to nod gravely to mere statesmen like Guizot when they craved permission to speak. For a short time the modest apartment in the rue d'Artois was again the rendezvous of a cultivated French society, but once more Madame de Vigny fell ill. The air of Paris did not agree with her so back they went to Maine Giraud. It was a tedious journey for Lydia did not like the railway and she could only travel a few hours a day by road. The increasing difficulty of finding reliable postillions added to the complications so that the migration sometimes took a week or ten days.

Lydia revived at Maine Giraud but gradually the heart attacks became more frequent and the convalescences more prolonged. Vigny was worried for fear the local doctors were making some mistake in their diagnosis. He began to feel that after all Lydia would be better off in Paris, but the prospect of leaving Maine Giraud which would have delighted him a few years earlier was now only a source of regret. The poor helpless Lydia who depended so utterly upon her husband had somehow contrived to infect him with her own simple love of the country. What was to have been a *pied à terre* for a few hot weeks in the summer or a convenient haven to take shelter in when the periodic revolutionary mania seized Paris had imperceptibly developed into a home.

Vigny was leading a richer and more varied life at Maine Giraud than he had ever enjoyed in Paris. At the same time his own health was almost as precarious as Lydia's. When he was still a young man he had been discharged from the army with chronic pneumonia and though he had outgrown that tendency he had already begun to suffer from a cancer of the stomach, which eventually caused his death. Under the circumstances it is not surprising that the business of travelling which our generation takes so lightly should have thrown the two invalids into something of a panic. One of Vigny's letters to his cousin the Vicomtesse de Plessis proves to what depths of gloom the postponement of a journey may give rise: " The trunks were packed and we were on the point of starting for Paris when your poor cousin was again taken ill. I am worried by this fever which comes and goes without rhyme or reason. The bloodletting is very weakening and it does no good. The doctors change the name of the illness without being able to cure it. . . . I give life and courage to every one around me which means pouring forth whatever natural gaiety there may be in my character; then when I am alone, as I am at this moment at midnight with the lamp as my only companion, sadness wells up in my heart and oppresses me to a degree that is almost intolerable. . . . In the intervals of my anguish I write, and I have here stored away in my hermitage a good many volumes ready for the printer as soon as our poor mad France is once more ready to read and to listen." If Vigny enjoyed his little wail no one can deny that he was entitled to it.

The last few years of their lives were spent almost entirely in Paris. As a conscientious academician Vigny devoted much of his time, too much perhaps, to reading the mass of second-rate poetry that is annually submitted for the various Academy prizes. He also took the elections very seriously and it was largely through his insistence that Alfred de Musset was allowed a place among the immortals. Musset was genuinely fond of Vigny even though he did describe him on one occasion as a '*vieil ange.*' If there is something ridiculous about being an antiquated angel at least it is not as bad as being a beautiful angel who has had the misfortune to drink vinegar, as Sainte-Beuve put it.

Another poet whom Vigny would have liked to see elected to the Academy was Baudelaire but he advised him against putting forward his name as he could not possibly have got the requisite number of votes. Vigny was one of the first and most enthusiastic admirers of ' Les Fleurs du Mal,' his only criticism being that the title was a misnomer. It should have been ' Les Fleurs du Bien.' The letters that passed between the two poets were not by any means confined to literary subjects. Baudelaire had a passion for prescribing drastic remedies for his friends' ailments. In one letter we find him urging Vigny to drink quantities of Bass' Ale which he had always found to be the panacea for every stomach complaint. Poor Vigny who had been reduced for the last two years of his life to a milk diet was in no condition to savor the excellence of Bass' Ale.

The most intimate friends of these years, however, were not young poets like Baudelaire or even seasoned men of letters like Busoni and Barbier, but a Jewish family named Franck who lived conveniently near Vigny in the rue de l'Oratoire. The Franck family consisted of Monsieur and Madame Adolphe Franck, two children whom he used to take to the theatre on every possible occasion, and a sister-in-law Delphine Bernard who was one of the many young ladies whom Vigny worshipped with tender respect. Delphine Bernard had every qualification for attracting him. Her name reminded him of his first love, she looked like a Raphael who was his favorite painter, and she was an artist in pastel a medium which he very much admired. She was young, she was talented and she was unworldly. Even if she had not been beautiful Vigny would have instinctively gravitated towards her. There is no figure in French literature comparable to Vigny in his attitude toward girlhood. There are plenty of passionate lovers and there are a few child-idolaters like Victor Hugo, though not so many as in English literature, but there is no one who revels in the society of ingénues except Vigny. Today when the intermediate stage between the innocence of childhood and the complete sophistication of the woman of the world is practically extinct Vigny's delight in the society of seventeen year old maidens is apt to be mistaken for the fatuousness of an elderly dandy. Perhaps when the quality of ingenuousness becomes fashionable again Vigny's attitude will be more comprehensible. For the moment it can only be understood by the exercise of the imagination.

After dinner, when his wife was asleep, Vigny would go over the household accounts for Lydia was quite incapable of attending to any business even when she was feeling well. Then he would drop in for a little conversation with his neighbors the Francks in the rue de l'Oratoire. There he was always sure to find agreeable company, and among others a certain Louis Ratisbonne who wound himself so effectually into Vigny's confidence that when Vigny died he was named as literary executor. Ratisbonne was another member of that chosen race to which Vigny was so strongly attracted at the end of his life. Was it that the Jews epitomized those qualities of abnegation and silent suffering that seemed to him the highest expression of the human spirit? Or did he feel some actual sympathy with the Hebrew faith? There was something almost Oriental in Vigny's ' patient deep disdain ' in the face of repeated disappointment. And yet the Jewish faith in Vigny's eyes was open to the same objections as Christianity. Neither religion was entirely disinterested. It was perhaps Buddhism that came nearest to satisfying his ideals. Six hundred years before Christ Buddha had offered the world a religion of love, he had advocated the monastic life, and above all he had taught the supreme value of sacrifice of oneself for others without hope of reward in a future life. That was a creed that made a powerful appeal to his stark ascetic spirit. The continuity of Catholicism attracted him as it must attract everybody with any sense of history, but the egoism of Christianity implied in the doctrine of the resurrection of the body was always a great stumbling block to him.

The urgency of the question of the future life came home to Vigny with particular force one afternoon in August, 1861. He had taken his usual walk with Louis Ratisbonne in the Bois de Boulogne. On returning home he was seized with convulsive pains such as he had never known before. For three weeks he was in bed practically without food, unable to read or write and quite incapable of looking after Lydia. Finally he rallied sufficiently to see a few of his friends and to resume his daily outings in the Bois, but old age had suddenly struck him with its thunderbolt. The busy farmer-poet-academician realized that he would never be active again. Books and talk were the only resources left. Vigny became more and more absorbed in questions of philosophy. Meanwhile his friends speculated whether he would make his peace with the Church. To the exhortations of the devout Louise Lachaud, the daughter of one of his oldest friends who had been brought up to believe only in God and Chateaubriand, he replies warning her that he may suddenly let loose upon her head ' un grand coup de raison ' which will shatter her comfortable little creed as the sword of Roland had shattered the ranks of the Saracens. When the Protestants on the other hand claim him as their own Vigny promptly falls back on the faith of his fathers: " I like being a Catholic," he replies in answer to their arguments, " for it is the religion in which the greater part of the world has died; it is always a comfort to be able to say that to oneself." Obviously he was not going to be stampeded into the fold but still less was he going to allow any heretical sect to claim him as their own.

Madame de Vigny cared for none of these things. She had been born a Protestant and a Protestant she remained. It no more occurred to her to speculate about religion than to attempt to share her husband's intellectual life. His companionship was everything to her and had been everything to her from the day they were married but it had never included adventuring in the world of ideas. As soon as he had sufficiently recovered from his illness he took up his post again at her bedside. He describes himself not without a touch of bitterness as ' un garde malade rêveur et voilà tout.' Actually he gloried in his abnegation. Lydia's complete dependence upon him brought out a vein of strength in his character that might otherwise never have come to light. The luxury of self-denial is only comprehended by a few but to those few the very bitterness of the sensation is curiously satisfying. Whereas the passion for Marie Dorval had left nothing behind but dust and ashes Vigny's devotion to his mother and to his wife, which had meant serious financial sacrifices, had yielded a

life-time of self-respect. As for his other affairs they
were too ephemeral to affect the fabric of his character. We can only suppose that the placid Lydia, if
she knew of her husband's infidelities at all, com-
forted herself with the reflection that his passing fan-
cies were not very flattering to the ladies involved.
The lines in ' Dolorida,' a poem written some years
before his marriage, proved strangely prophetic:

> *Je jure que jamais mon amour egarée*
> *N'oublia loin de toi ton image adorée;*
> *L'infidélité même était pleine de toi,*
> *Je te voyais partout entre ma faute et moi. . . .*

> I swear that though my fancy wandered
> Our souls have never dwelt apart;
> Faithless, your precious love I squandered,
> Yet 'twas your image filled my heart. . . .

After thirty-five years of intermittent ill health
Lydia's death was mercifully sudden. One afternoon
in December, 1862, she and Vigny had gone out to
watch the balloon ascensions, one of the popular di-
versions of the Parisian in the 'sixties. Just as they
were returning home she collapsed from heart failure. The fatal stroke dreaded for so many years had
come at last. She died almost immediately in Vigny's
arms. " Mon bon Alfred, je ne souffre pas." That was
his only consolation. The docile loving creature for
whom he had sacrificed so much had become far
more essential to him than his friends imagined. He
had stood between her and death for so many years

that now that death had finally wrested her from him he felt more than ever bereft. His cousin, the Vicomtesse de Plessis, offered to come and see him but for the moment he wanted no companionship. Like a wounded animal he craved only to be left alone. A few months after Lydia's death thinking probably that his grief had spent itself the Vicomtesse wrote him one of her frivolous letters about the dances she was going to and gay world she was seeing, but Vigny was not to be amused. " If I have not answered your last letter, my dear Alexandrine, it is because there is such a cruel contrast between my sufferings, mental and physical, and the thoughtless frivolity of your letters that I thought it better to leave you in peace to the enjoyment of your butterfly existence." Obviously M. de Vigny was not to be distracted from his grief. After all, the man who has just lost the companion of nearly forty years and who is himself suffering agonies of pain from a cancer of the stomach may well be excused for resenting such clumsy consolation as his cousin offered him.

In the last few months of his life Vigny recovered something of his old serenity. The ghastly callousness of the undertakers, who made their way to his bedside to deliver their bill, infuriated him but once the funeral was over his cherished stoicism came to the rescue. Though he was unable to leave his room he was as alive as ever to the consolation offered by his favorite authors. Shakespeare's historical plays and Goethe's ' Elective Affinities ' were the last books that he read. The end came on September 16, 1863. The physical agony was almost more than he could bear. " Pray for me, pray to God for me," he kept on whispering to his friends. On the night of the fifteenth the Abbé Vidal administered extreme unction. Afterwards he drank a little milk which seemed to revive him. The pain ceased and it looked as if he might linger on for a few days but suddenly the soul fluttered away as if set free by the loosening of the bonds of pain.

Vigny was born a Catholic and at the end of his life he reverted instinctively to the old faith. Louis Ratisbonne maintains that he received the visits of a priest like the gentleman that he was but that he never confessed to him. This assertion is flatly contradicted by the Abbé Vidal, also by Madame d'Orville, an old family friend, who states that Vigny not only confessed but added in a clear enough voice to be heard in the next room: " je suis né catholique et je meurs catholique." It is not unnatural that an anticlerical like Ratisbonne should wish to claim Vigny as one of the great rebels against the tyranny of the Church, or that the Abbé Vidal should be equally anxious to prove that in his last days Vigny regretted his intellectual arrogance and made his submission like a good Catholic. Vigny would probably have smiled and let them both have it their own way. We have seen that he was too much afflicted with the uneasy passion for liberty to be thoroughly at home in the Catholic Church but he was equally too intelligent to ignore the tremendous debt, moral, aesthetic and intellectual, that civilization owes to Catholicism. He had given a statue of the Virgin to the country church near Maine Giraud and he had been made godfather, a curious title, to the church bells. He had always been on excellent terms with the local clergy. On the other hand he had written certain lines, particularly the epilogue to ' Le Mont des Oliviers ' in which he rebukes God for his indifference, which are almost blasphemous. He could never reconcile Christianity with the damning fact of unjustified suffering. The touching faith implied in the cry ' Lord I believe, help thou mine unbelief ' was something to which he could never attain, and yet it was equally out of the question for a man of Vigny's spiritual texture to brush past Christianity and live by philosophy alone.

One of Vigny's contemporaries is guilty of an epigram at his expense which has so often been repeated that it has come to be regarded as the essential clue to his character. His successor in the Academy was regretting that he had not known him better, upon which Jules Sandeau remarked: ' You may console yourself, Vigny was not on intimate terms with anybody not even with himself.' From this epigram and from Sainte-Beuve's phrase about the ivory tower has sprung the legend that Vigny was a disgruntled aristocrat, a Horace without Horace's serenity who battened on his own society and prided himself on his hatred of the common herd. Nothing could be more inaccurate. Vigny took the keenest interest in contemporary affairs. He was a practical man of business, a conscientious landlord, and a most affectionate friend. As for living on intimate terms with himself, whatever that may mean, he had certainly based his whole life on a code of behavior carefully thought out and conscientiously executed. It was only when he had fulfilled every obligation towards the world that he allowed himself to seek the ivory tower. Had he been more selfish and less willing to tilt at injustice wherever it raised its head, he might have written more novels like 'Stello' and more poems like 'La Maison du Berger.' As it was, his primary concern in life was moral rather than literary. The question of how life should be lived rather than how it should be recorded was what really interested him. The last entry in the journal is strangely significant:

"It has been said that the ancient peoples of the north believed that in the next world they would find their ancestors gathered together in large caves, seated on thrones and plunged in mute deliberation since they only communicated with each other by thought. When a new arrival who had distinguished himself in the world presented himself before this mysterious gathering they would all rise and bow before him. The memory of this superstition which was believed perhaps by the Franks, the forefathers of my forefathers, has always appealed to me on account of its sombre grandeur. More than once I have acted or abstained from acting in a certain way because I suddenly remembered the judgment of this supreme council, of these dumb spirits, sitting with their hands on their knees like the gods of Egypt, and I have said to myself: ' I ought to live in such a way as to make them stand up when I join their company.' "

Vigny need have no fears. On the day of judgment his ancestors will stand up when he joins their company, not merely because he ' made illustrious an unknown name,' but because in his stoicism he represented the finest expression of the pagan spirit, and because in his charity and kindliness he had stumbled upon the essence of Christianity.

BIBLIOGRAPHY AND NOTES

I have deliberately avoided the use of asterisks and footnotes in the belief that in a book of this kind the apparatus of scholarship should be kept separate from the text. The following notes, however, may be useful to those who wish to consult for themselves the authorities upon which this study is based. I am indebted to Professor Hoffherr of Columbia University for reading the proof and to Miss Elizabeth Bethel for preparing the index.

The greatest living authority on Alfred de Vigny is Professor Fernand Baldensperger. His edition of the complete works of Vigny with Notes et Eclaircissements is published by Conard, Paris, 1913–1933. Unfortunately the last two volumes of this edition containing Vigny's correspondence were not published until after this book was in the press.

Vigny's 'Journal d'un Poète,' also edited by Prof. Baldensperger, was published by the Scholartis Press, London, 1928. The previous edition of this journal was notoriously incomplete. Vigny now takes his place beside Leopardi, Senancour, and Amiel, as one of that small group of romantic writers who produced books of confession that were not inspired by motives of bravado or self-justification but simply by the desire to examine their own ideas honestly and dispassionately. The notion that the author of such a book must necessarily have lived in an ivory tower has been effectually destroyed by Prof. Baldensperger who has cleared away so many of the cobwebs encrusted around Vigny's reputation. I should like to take this occasion to express my indebtedness to this great scholar who has allowed so many students to profit by his researches. It was owing to his kindness that I obtained access to the Collection Lovenjoul in the Musée de Chantilly.

Vigny has been the subject of innumerable biographies, essays, and dissertations. An extensive bibliography will be found in ' La Pensée Politique et Sociale d'Alfred de Vigny' by P. Flottes, Paris, 1927. Curiously enough he has not attracted as much attention from English or American scholars as might be expected considering his vogue in the class room.

A good account of his life and times will be found in Ernest Dupuy's ' Alfred de Vigny. Ses Amitiés, Son Rôle littéraire,' 2 vols., Paris, 1912, and in Léon Séché's ' Alfred de Vigny,' 2 vols., Paris, 1913. These are hardly biographies in the modern sense of the word but they contain a mass of information not readily obtainable elsewhere.

A very readable monograph on Vigny was written by Anatole France as long ago as 1868. It is not free from inaccuracies but it is interesting as being the first biography of Vigny and the first prose work from the pen of Anatole France.

M. Maurice Paléologue is the author of the excellent volume on Vigny in 'les grands ecrivains de France' series, Paris, 1891.

Among the best of the recent biographies is the little volume by Robert de Traz in a series entitled 'Les Romantiques,' Paris, 1928.

Sainte-Beuve's essays on Vigny shed almost as much light on Sainte-Beuve as they do upon Vigny. It must be remembered that he was not fond of Vigny, but his criticism is always penetrating and his admiration of Vigny the poet is proof against his dislike for Vigny the man. For Sainte-Beuve's final estimate see the essay in the Nouveaux Lundis, vol. VI, written shortly after Vigny's death. A review of 'Servitude et Grandeur Militaires' will be found in the second volume of the Portraits Contemporains, and a severe criticism of his address before the Academy in the Portraits Littéraires, vol. 111.

The essay on Vigny by Paul Bourget (Etudes et Portraits, vol. 1, Paris, 1888) is an admirable starting point for the understanding and appreciation of Vigny's poetry.

English readers will be interested in the essay by Edmund Gosse (French Profiles, London, 1905) which emphasizes Vigny's Anglophile tendencies.

Among the books addressed to the specialist of Vigny rather than to the general reader I have found the following works particularly useful.

F. Baldensperger. A. de Vigny; contribution à sa biographie intellectuelle. Paris. 1912.

Pierre Flottes. La Pensée Politique et Sociale d'Alfred de Vigny. Paris. 1927.

BIBLIOGRAPHY AND NOTES

M. CITOLEUX. A. de Vigny; persistances classiques et affinites etrangeres. Paris. 1924.

E. ESTEVE. Les Destinées. Edition critique. Paris. 1923.

CHAPTER I

PAGE 1. The best account of the consternation caused by the news of Napoleon's return from Elba is contained in H. Houssaye's ' 1815.' 3 vols. (Paris.) See vol. 1, p. 354 et seq.

PAGE 2. One of the aspects of war that has never been studied is the devastating effect that it has upon the schoolroom. See the first chapter of Vigny's ' Servitude et Grandeur,' Musset's ' La Confession d'un Enfant du Siècle,' ch. 2, and Michelet's ' Ma Jeunesse,' ch. 9. Many men who were schoolmasters 1914–1918 can bear witness to the difficulty of teaching history while the fathers and brothers of every boy in the school were busy making it.

PAGE 9. Frederick Masson contributed an interesting account of the history of the Elysée Bourbon to Le Temps, April 28, 1900.

PAGE 13. Victor Hugo's impression of school life will be found in his ' Rayons et Ombres,' no. XIX. Lamartine's description of his lycée is even more gloomy. See ' Mes Confidences,' Book VI.

CHAPTER II

The effect of army life upon Alfred de Vigny is fully discussed in Captain Marabail's ' De l'Influence de l'Esprit Militaire sur l'oeuvre d'Alfred de Vigny.' (Paris. 1905.)

BIBLIOGRAPHY AND NOTES

PAGE 23. The quotation is taken from 'Servitude et Grandeur Militaires,' Part I, chapter 3.

PAGE 26. See Vigny's letter to Louise Lachaud, dated 1847. — "Il faut que vous sachiez, vous, Louise, que toutes les fois que dans ce livre de Servitude et Grandeur militaires, il y a: 'je,' c'est la vérité."

PAGE 29. The 'Journal d'un Poète' contains several autobiographical fragments entitled 'Fragments de Mémoires.' This quotation will be found on p. 241.

PAGE 29. Madame de Vigny's copy of 'Héléna' is preserved in the Collection Lovenjoul in the Musée de Chantilly.

PAGE 33. A new edition of 'La Muse Française' edited by Jules Marsan was published in 1907, Paris.

PAGE 33. The authoritative life of Emile Deschamps, 'Un bourgeois romantique' by E. Girard (Paris, 1921), throws considerable light on this period of Vigny's life.

PAGE 35. The quotation is taken from Dumas' 'Mémoires' (Paris, 1896), vol. 5, p. 283.

PAGE 37. Marcel Bouteron, the great authority on Balzac, has an interesting account of 'Les Muses Romantiques' in *La Revue Hebdomadaire,* March–April, 1926. See also 'Portraits et Salons Romantiques' by Lamartine, edited with an introduction by Louis Barthou, Paris, 1927.

PAGE 41. For further details about Vigny's life at Pau see P. Lafond's 'Alfred de Vigny en Béarn.'

PAGE 42. See 'Lettres inédites d'Alfred de Vigny à Victor Hugo,' Paris, 1925, edited by Louis Barthou.

Presumably these letters are included in Baldensperger's complete edition.

PAGE 43. Victor Hugo had written a poem entitled 'La fille d'Otaiti' which Vigny apparently had just been reading.

PAGE 45. See 'Le Journal d'un Poète,' p. 59 and p. 67.

CHAPTER III

Excellent illustrations of the Paris of this period will be found in Philip Carr's 'Days with the French Romantics.' (London. 1932.)

PAGE 51. See Dumas' charming description of Charles Nodier and the soirées at the Arsenal in his 'Memoires,' vol. 5, pp. 116–130. Also 'Charles Nodier et le Groupe Romantique' by Michel Salomon. (Paris. 1908.)

PAGE 54. 'Paris and the Parisians in 1835' by Mrs. Trollope. (London. 1836.) vol. 1, p. 276.

PAGE 55. 'France in 1829–1830' by Lady Morgan. 2 vols. (London. 1830.) vol. 1, p. 209.

PAGE 56. 'Celebrities and I' by Henrietta Corkran. (London. 1902.)

PAGE 57. Theodore de Banville's 'Souvenirs,' p. 44. (Paris. 1882.)

PAGE 60. 'Mes Souvenirs' by Madame d'Agoult (Paris. 1877) contains interesting anecdotes about Vigny. See also her recently published correspondence with Liszt. (Paris. 1932.)

PAGE 61. Vigny tells the story of his visit to Sir Walter Scott in 'Le Journal d'un Poète,' p. 8. Scott's influence upon the French novel has been traced by Louis Maigron. ' Le roman historique à l'époque romantique.' (Paris. 1912.)

Page 65. See ' Sainte-Beuve et Alfred de Vigny ' by Louis Gillet. (Paris. 1929.)

Page 68. The stanza quoted is from Sainte-Beuve's poem Le Cénacle.

Page 70. A description of Vigny at one of these soirées will be found in A. Barbier's ' Souvenirs Personnels.' (Paris. 1883.)

Chapter IV

For the growth of the Shakespeare in France see J. J. Jusserand's ' Shakespeare in France under the Ancien Regime.' (London. 1899.) Also F. Baldensperger's ' Esquisse d'une histoire de Shakespeare en France ' (Etudes d'histoire littéraire. vol. 2, Paris. 1910.)

Page 73. See particularly letter 18 in the ' Lettres Philosophiques.'

Page 77. Dumas claims that it was Shakespeare who decided the course of his life. See his article in *La Revue des Deux Mondes* (1833) . ' Comment je devins un auteur dramatique.'

Page 85. See S. P. E. Tract No. XVII. Four Words: Romantic, Originality, Creative, Genius. By Logan Pearsall Smith. (Oxford. 1924.)

Page 86. See Guizot's ' Shakespeare et son Temps.' (Paris. 1852.)

BIBLIOGRAPHY AND NOTES

CHAPTER V

A good account of the founding of *La Revue des Deux Mondes* can be found in M. L. Pailleron's 'François Buloz et ses Amis.' (Paris. 1919.)

PAGE 96. These lines appear in the 'Journal d'un Poète,' p. 24. Vigny never reprinted them.

PAGE 99. Vigny's knowledge of Collingwood was acquired from 'A Selection from the public and private Correspondence of Vice-Admiral Lord Collingwood; interspersed with Memoirs of his Life' by G. L. Newham Collingwood. (London. 1828.)

PAGE 103. There is a good essay on Mademoiselle George in Clement-Janin's 'Drames et Comédies Romantiques.' (Paris. 1928.) Further details will be found in Dumas' 'Mes Mémoires,' vol. 5, p. 306.

CHAPTER VI

Marie Dorval's biographers have all profited by the excellent chapter devoted to her in George Sand's 'Histoire de ma Vie.' (Paris. 1856.) Book IX, pp. 120–164. Dumas' 'Mémoires,' from which I have quoted extensively (vol. 7, p. 176) show another side of her character. See also the notice on Marie Dorval in Théophile Gautier's 'Histoire du Romantisme.'

PAGE 112. 'Journal d'un Poète,' p. 114.

PAGE 119. The quotation from Vigny's letter to Marie Dorval will be found in Leon Séché's 'Alfred de Vigny,' vol. 2, p. 151.

BIBLIOGRAPHY AND NOTES

Chapter VII

PAGE 132. Letter to the Vicomtesse du Plessis, October 7, 1849.

PAGE 136. The details of Vigny's lawsuit will be found in Doris Gunnell's 'Sutton Sharpe et ses amis français.' (Paris. 1926.) The best source of information on Vigny's English friends is Ernest Dupuy. See his life of Vigny, vol. I, p. 49 et seq. Also an article on the same subject in the *Mercure de France*. (June 1, 1909.)

PAGE 138. Quoted from the 'Journal d'un Poète,' p. 94.

PAGE 140. See the 'New Letters of Thomas Carlyle' edited by Alex. Carlyle. (London. 1904.) Vol. I, p. 150.

PAGE 143. Macready's 'Diary and Reminiscences' contains several references to Vigny indicating that they were on the pleasantest terms.

PAGE 144. See 'Lettres Inédites d'Alfred de Vigny au Marquis et à la Marquise de la Grange,' edited by A. de Luppé. (Paris. 1914) p. 37.

PAGE 145. Letter to Mrs. Austen, March 26, 1841.

PAGE 146. See Henrietta Corkran — 'Celebrities and I.' (London. 1902.)

PAGE 147. Some of Vigny's letters to Camilla Maunoir were published in the Revue de Paris (August 15 and September 15, 1897).

PAGE 149. Quotation from the 'Journal d'un Poète,' p. 191.

CHAPTER VIII

PAGE 151. 'Dix Ans après en littérature' will be found in the 'Portraits Contemporains,' vol. 2.

PAGE 153. This incident is discussed at some length in M. Souriau's 'Moralistes et Poètes.' (Paris. 1907.)

PAGE 156. The proclamation to the electors of the Charente is quoted in the appendix of the A. de Vigny 'Correspondance' edited by E. Sakellarides. Paris. n.d.

PAGE 157. The story of the struggle for the Academy is told in the 'Journal d'un Poète,' p. 162 et seq. See also 'Les Romantiques à l'Académie' by Paul Souday. (Paris. 1928.)

PAGE 162. Proust's reference to Vigny will be found in 'A l'ombre des jeunes filles en fleurs,' p. 23. (Paris. 1925.)

PAGE 165. The only authority I have been able to find for Jules Clarétie's accusation is 'Les Nouvelles Littéraires,' March 25, 1933.

PAGE 167. For Lamartine's estimate of Vigny see his 'Cours familier de littérature,' vol. XVI, p. 410.

CHAPTER IX

PAGE 168. Croce's essay on Vigny will be found in his 'European Literature in the XIX Century,' translated by Douglas Ainslie. (London. 1924.)

PAGE 172. The quotation is from 'La Maison du Berger':

Ne me laisse jamais seul avec la Nature
Car je la connais trop pour n'en avoir pas peur.

BIBLIOGRAPHY AND NOTES

PAGE 173. Daphné was first published in 1913 with an introduction by Fernan Gregh. In Baldensperger's edition it appears in the same volume with Stello.

PAGE 174. Pierre Lasserre, an unsparing critic of romanticism, has an interesting though unsympathetic chapter on Vigny's pessimism in his 'Le Romantisme Français.' (Paris. 1907.)

PAGE 174. The quotation about solitude is from the 'Journal d'un Poète,' p. 74.

PAGE 179. For Thiers' attitude towards the railroads see 'France under the Bourbon Restoration' by Frederick B. Artz. (Harvard University Press) 1931.

CHAPTER X

PAGE 188. For an account of Vigny's relations with Louise Colet see the article by Prof. Strowski in *La Revue des Cours et des Conférences* (1923), p. 1083.

PAGE 190. Vigny's life at La Maine Giraud is dealt with in 'La Forteresse Charentaise d'Alfred de Vigny' by Pierre du Chambon. (Ruffec. 1931.) The house itself, now the property of M. Phelipon, is still the charming little 'gentilhommière' that it was in Vigny's day, but the surrounding forests have disappeared.

PAGE 195. An article by François Porché, based on these letters, will be found in 'Les Nouvelles Littéraires,' June 6, 1931.

PAGE 200. Vigny's relations with Busoni, Barbier and Brizeux, are dealt with at length by Dupuy and Séché.

BIBLIOGRAPHY AND NOTES

PAGE 203. See Vigny's letter to the Vicomtesse de Plessis, March 11, 1852.

PAGE 204. See 'Alfred de Vigny et Charles Baudelaire' by E. Charavary. (Paris. 1879.)

PAGE 205. There is a chapter on the Franck family in Séché, vol. 2, p. 240.

PAGE 206. For Vigny's interest in Buddhism see 'L'Orientalisme d'Alfred de Vigny' by Vera A. Summers. (Paris. 1930.)

PAGE 210. See Vigny's letter to the Vicomtesse de Plessis, April 2, 1863.

PAGE 212. Sainte-Beuve's celebrated phrase about the ivory tower occurs in a poem addressed to Villemain published in the volume of his poetry entitled 'Pensées d'août.'

INDEX

INDEX

INDEX

INDEX

INDEX

INDEX

This book was composed, printed, and bound by the Plimpton Press, Norwood, Massachusetts.

The typographical arrangement, binding and jacket designs are by Mr. W. A. Dwiggins.